NO OTHER NAME

SYNCRETISM. Attempted union or reconciliation of diverse or opposite tenets or practices, especially in philosophy or religion.

Oxford English Dictionary

By the name of Jesus Christ of Nazareth, whom you crucified, whom God raised from the dead, by him this man is standing before you well.

And there is salvation in no one else, for there is no other name under heaven given among men by which we must be saved.

Acts 4.10, 12 (RSV)

NO OTHER NAME

*The choice between syncretism and
Christian Universalism*

❊

W. A. Visser 't Hooft

The Westminster Press

PHILADELPHIA

Books by W. A. Visser 't Hooft
published by The Westminster Press

No Other Name
Rembrandt and the Gospel
The Renewal of the Church

CONTENTS

Preface   7

I   SYNCRETISM—ANCIENT AND
    MODERN   9
    The first wave of syncretism   12
    The second wave of syncretism   14
    The third wave of syncretism   22
    The fourth wave of syncretism   28
    Eastern syncretism   35
    Syncretistic movements and sects   41

II THE NEW TESTAMENT'S
    STRUGGLE WITH SYNCRETISM   50
    Some early conflicts with syncretism   54
    Is New Testament terminology syncretistic?   62
    The answer to syncretism in confession and
        mission   74
    Did syncretism prepare the way for
        Christianity?   76
    Is the New Testament a product of
        syncretism?   77

III ONE FOR ALL AND ONCE
    FOR ALL   83
    The argument for cultural understanding   83
    The search for a common world faith   86

Syncretism's challenge to Christianity	92
What is Christian universalism?	96
The rediscovery of Christocentric universalism in the ecumenical movement	103
The answer to syncretism and its implications:	
(a) For the nature of a true universalism	113
(b) For our attitude to the religions	116
(c) For collaboration in common tasks	119
(d) For the communication of the Gospel	122
(e) For the life of the Church	124
Index of names	126

ABBREVIATIONS

ET	English translation
HNT	Handbuch zum Neuen Testament, Tübingen
NEB	New English Bible, New Testament
RSV	Revised Standard Version of the Bible
TWNT	*Theologisches Wörterbuch zum Neuen Testament,* ed. G. Kittel, Stuttgart, 1932ff.

PREFACE

MOST OF the material in this book was used for the Charles Hein lectures which I gave in April and May 1962 at the theological seminaries of the American Lutheran Church in Columbus, Dubuque and St Paul. The third chapter was also used for lectures at the Rassemblement Protestant in Lausanne, at the meeting of the commission on missions of the Lutheran World Federation in 1962, at the University of Helsinki and at Princeton Theological Seminary.

I have chosen this particular subject because I feel that we need greater clarity on the nature of syncretism and on the attitude which the ecumenical movement should adopt to it. Unable to find books which answered the questions I had in mind I came to the conclusion that I would have to try to work out the answer myself. I realize of course that I am in no sense an expert in the areas of history or biblical theology and that I have had to depend on others who have done the primary research.

Since I wrote most of these lectures the situation has changed in that two friends and colleagues have published books which deal to a large extent with the same subject matter. I refer to Lesslie Newbigin's *A Faith for this one World?* (SCM Press) and to Hendrik Kraemer's *World Cultures and World Religions* (Lutterworth Press). I hope that many readers will read those books together with mine. They will find that although the approaches differ, we three arrive at the same fundamental conclusions. I must add the customary, but not unimportant warning, that the opinions expressed in this book are not to be taken as the opinions of the World Council of Churches, but simply as those of one of its many servants.

Geneva, October 1962

I

SYNCRETISM—ANCIENT
AND MODERN

I S I T wise to raise the issue of syncretism to-day? Are we not at a moment of history in which the real line of demarcation runs between religion and atheism? Is that not a bad moment to speak critically of the various attempts to mix different religions? Should we not rather defend the common religious front in every form and at any price?

The main theme of these lectures is that this is precisely the time to confront the fundamental question of syncretism. We must do so in order to ensure that the religion we defend has real integrity. We must do so especially as Christians because there is real danger that we may find ourselves before long exceedingly rich in religion and exceedingly poor in real Christianity.

No one can deny that we have reason to be worried about the tremendous strides of secularism and the emergence of masses which seem to have lost all contact with religion in any form. But does not all that we know about man and about history tell us that man cannot for long live the completely godless life? And are we so sure that these men and women who do not appear in our churches are really irreligious? Are they not at the same time the readers of the masses of cheap literature about religions old and new or of poetry and novels which advocate some special new brand of religiosity? Our time is not only an epoch of atheism but equally of astounding curiosity about religious matters. But the great question is whether all this seeking will lead us more deeply into spiritual chaos and confusion or whether it will lead to a true renewal of faith.

There is this further reason why this is the time to speak of the problem of syncretism. Many of the best among us are deeply anxious about the inability of the human family, now forced for better or worse to live in close contact, to find a common ethos, a common standard for human relations. It is realized that such an ethos must be rooted in common convictions about the ultimate issues of life. Does it not follow that we must somehow force the religious leaders to come to agreement and to develop one universal world-religion? Is therefore syncretism in some form not inevitable?

It is precisely this plausible, rationally almost self-evident character of the syncretistic answer to the needs of the world that makes it a far more dangerous challenge to the Christian Church than full-fledged atheism is ever likely to be. For those who are in any sense believing Christians a purely materialistic view of life is not a serious temptation. But the same cannot be said of systems of thought which seem only to add a wider dimension to the faith of the Church.

Our task in this lecture is to describe the various forms which syncretism has taken in history and which it takes to-day. But before we do so we have to give a provisional definition of the meaning of syncretism. The word has been used in various senses. Some speak of syncretism whenever a particular religion makes any use of concepts which have their origin in the life of another religion. But in that case we would have to conclude that every religion which steps out of its original environment is syncretistic, because it is quite impossible to enter into communication with people who live in another environment without using expressions and concepts which are in some way related to and embedded in the religious world in which the people concerned are living. Translation is *not* syncretism, if it is done with the desire to pass on the original message as clearly as possible and without greater modification of its original content than is inevitable in any process of translation.

Others speak of syncretism when a particular religion goes further than translation and takes into its own life ideas or practices which have their origin in another religious world. But this is also a too general use of the word. For every world-religion has done so. The great question is whether the 'foreign' elements become a part of the original structure or whether that structure is essentially modified by them. Absorption, as Dr Kraemer has pointed out, is not syncretism when it is undertaken with a sense of clear discrimination and when 'rites and conceptions of different origin and of a different degree of affinity have been adapted to its dominant spirit and concern in such a way that they have become a genuine and accepted part of this religion'.[1]

The word syncretism should be reserved for another type of religious attitude, which deserves to have its own name because it is such an important, persistent and widespread religious phenomenon. This is the view which holds that there is no unique revelation in history, that there are many different ways to reach the divine reality, that all formulations of religious truth or experience are by their very nature inadequate expressions of that truth and that it is necessary to harmonize as much as possible all religious ideas and experiences so as to create one universal religion for mankind. Professor Oepke puts the matter clearly: 'Real syncretism is always based on the presupposition that all positive religions are only reflections of a universal original religion (*Urreligion*) and show therefore only gradual differences.'[2] It is in this sense that we will use the word in these lectures. This means that we do not accept the ter-

[1] H. Kraemer, *Religion and the Christian Faith*, 1956, p. 397.
[2] A. Oepke, *Das neue Gottesvolk*, 1950, p. 124.

minology of men like von Harnack[3] and Bultmann who use one and the same word 'syncretism' for such basically different phenomena as the 'theocrasia', the mixture and fusion of the gods in the Roman Empire, on the one hand and the assimilation by the Christian Church of concepts borrowed from the Mediterranean religious and cultural environment on the other hand.

The first wave of syncretism

We must now make a rapid survey of the history of syncretism in its bearing upon the life of the Church. We can distinguish four great syncretistic waves.

The first great syncretistic crisis which belongs to the history of the Christian Church as well as to that of Israel took place in the last century before the Exile. There was, of course, nothing new in the fact that the prophets of the God of Moses had to fight idolatry. What was new was that idolatry no longer appeared in the naive form of ancient popular religion, but in the sophisticated form and with the prestige of the magnificent and powerful Babylonian-Assyrian culture. From the point of view of political realism it is not surprising that King Manasseh considered it expedient to underline his attachment to the Assyrian ideology. He was only making the mistake which so many politicians have made when in order to save the existence of their nation they proved ready to give up the *raison d'être* of that nation. Manasseh tried to play the game, and that game was all over Western Asia the game of syncretism.

This time the foreign cults are introduced into the temple of Jerusalem itself. And that can only mean that while Yahweh continues to be worshipped, he is no longer considered as the one and only God in whose hands is the destiny of Israel; instead he is conceived as part of the vast

[3] Especially in his *The Expansion of Christianity* (ET, 1904-05).

pantheon in which there are only relative differences between the various gods. We hear during that period of worship of the sun, that is, the Babylonian Shamas with his sun-chariot (II Kings 23.11), of the image of Asherah, no doubt to be identified with Astarte (II Kings 21.3), of the Queen of Heaven, the Mother Goddess who represents life-giving Nature (Jer. 7.18; 44.17), and of Tammuz, the Babylonian form of the dying and rising Adonis (Ezek. 8.14). That such divinities are worshipped in and around the temple of Jerusalem, as is reported by the author of Kings, by Jeremiah and Ezekiel, shows that the God of Israel is in danger of being swallowed up by that pervasive, all-embracing nature-worship which is the common substructure, the religion within the religions of the Western Asian culture, a cult of which it has rightly been said that 'its roots were in the earth and of the earth'.[4] How earthly it is, is illustrated by the role which sex plays in this syncretism. Sacred prostitution has been introduced into the temple of Jerusalem itself (II Kings 23.7). Thus when Jeremiah (2.20) and Ezekiel (16.15ff.) compare Israel to a harlot they are not speaking only allegorically.

It is inadequate to describe the prophetic protest against this syncretism as a moral protest. It is far more. It is the refusal in the name of the living God who calls men by their name and demands their personal response, to let men become playthings of the dark, arbitrary forces of nature, the denial of the idea that man's ultimate destiny is to adjust himself to and let himself be integrated with the unending circular process of life and death represented by nature.

The sharpness of the prophetic reaction to this syncretistic crisis as we have it in Deuteronomy, in Jeremiah, in Ezekiel, is therefore not an exhibition of fanatical intoler-

[4] S. H. Hooke in *A Companion to the Bible*, ed. T. W. Manson, 1939, p. 286.

ance, but an expression of the deep insight and conviction that to mix the worship of Yahweh with the worship of other gods is in fact to deny the specific claim which the God of Israel makes. 'To you [Israel] it was shown that you might know that the Lord is God; there is no other beside him' (Deut. 4.35). Israel cannot and must not get away from the fact of the Exodus and the Covenant. And that fact means that it has met the one God who claims its total and exclusive allegiance. It can only lose, not gain, by drinking the waters of the Nile or of the Euphrates (Jer. 2.18). Syncretism is in its case impoverishment, degeneration (Jer. 2.21), total confusion (Jer. 2.23). It cannot afford to take the sophisticated attitude that one god is as good as another and that 'names are sound and smoke' (Faust) without losing its identity and its specific mission. We can never be grateful enough to Israel that it let itself be called back from the brink of the abyss.

The second wave of syncretism

The second wave of syncretism is the most formidable and comprehensive movement of intermingling and combination of diverse religions that has ever existed in history. This syncretism which found its climax in the days of the Roman Empire has been so fully described by such scholars as Cumont, Lietzmann, Nock, Wendland, Prümm that its main features are well known. For our purpose we need only call attention to some of its aspects which help to understand the general character of syncretism and which explain the reaction of the Christian Church to it.

We have to do with a movement which began when Alexander the Great laid the foundations for the emergence of an *oikoumene*, the antique parallel to our 'one world' concept, the new dynamic civilization, the parts of which are forced out of their isolation and drawn into a process of general cultural exchange. For about 700 years, that is from the time of Alexander to the time of St Augustine, the religions invade each other's territory, transform each other and become inextricably mixed up with each other.

The geographical scope of the process is immense. Isis and Sarapis with their Egyptian background, Cybele and Attis from Syria, Mithra whose origin lies in Persia, find their way not only to Rome, but to the frontiers of Germany and Britain.[5] 'From the banks of the Black Sea to the mountains of Scotland and to the borders of the great Sahara Desert, along the entire length of the Roman frontier, Mithraic monuments abound.'[6] And the oriental cults have not only attracted the Roman occupation armies, but found their way to the native population.

What does it all mean? Is it just a time of total religious confusion and complete lack of any sense of spiritual discrimination? That is indeed our first impression. When we hear that the Emperor Alexander Severus had in his private chapel not only the statues of the deified emperors, but also those of the miracle-worker Apollonius of Tyana, of Christ, of Abraham and of Orpheus, we wonder whether this man's faith had any recognizable substance. Of another emperor, Julian, it was said that he 'consorted with *daimones* in countless rites',[7] and we have the record of many of these initiations. Apuleius says of himself that he 'learnt worship on worship, rites beyond number'.[8] This sounds almost as if he collected religious experiences as philatelists collect stamps to-day. There are examples of attempts at synthesis of beliefs which are as radically divergent as any beliefs can be. I think especially of the astonishing identification of the Phrygian Dionysos Sabazios, one of the most char-

[5] F. Cumont, *The Oriental Religions in Roman Paganism*, ET, 1911, p. 22.
[6] F. Cumont, *The Mysteries of Mithra*, ET, 1910 (reprinted 1956), p. 43.
[7] A. D. Nock, *Conversion*, 1933 (reprinted 1961), p. 115.
[8] *Ibid.*, p. 114.

15

acteristic expressions of a purely naturalistic religion, with *Kyrios Sabaoth*, as the Septuagint calls the God of Israel.[9] Here syncretism celebrates its greatest triumph: to bring together the Holy God, the Creator before whom the worship of the creation is abhorrent and a god whose very *raison d'être* is to represent the self-sufficiency of creation. Yes, it is a scene of extraordinary confusion. Nevertheless it is possible to recognize certain factors which determine the whole process and make it at least partly intelligible.

The starting point is that, as A. D. Nock has made very clear, the ingredients of this syncretism are not convictions, but attitudes, not religions with a creed and a churchly structure, but rites 'efficient in themselves as rites and not as the expression of a theology and world-order sharply contrasted with those in which the neophyte had previously moved'.[10] The gods are various superhuman forces to be used. If there is an immutable and eternal ultimate reality, it is unknowable. So it is surely best to take advantage of the available opportunities to participate in the life of the gods through worship, sacrifice or even full initiation into their mysteries. We find that it is not just religious curiosity and dilettantism when countless men and women go from one temple to another, from one mystery cult to the next. Praetextatus, prefect of Rome in the fourth century, was considered in his days the great specialist on religions and philosophical affairs and he was certainly a man of remarkable sincerity. When he died, his wife wrote an epitaph in which she expressed her gratitude to him for having made her a servant of the gods and for having initiated her *in all mysteries*, specially those of Cybele, Hecate, and Eleusis.[11] Another high civil servant, Aedesius, presents himself in

[9] F. Cumont, *Oriental Religions*, p. 64.

[10] H. Lietzmann, *The Beginnings of the Christian Church* (History of the Early Church I), ET, 3rd ed., 1953, p. 161.

[11] Gaston Boissier, *La Fin du Paganisme* II, 1894, p. 264; K. Latte, *Die Religion der Römer* (Religionsg. Lesebuch), 2nd ed., 1927, p. 88.

an inscription of the same period as chief priest of Mithra, hierophant of Hecate, chief shepherd of Dionysus, born again through the taurobolium.[12]

It was of course inevitable that such syncretism in high places should lead among the less cultured to an indiscriminate acceptance of all forms of religious life, however bizarre and however crude. The religious frauds had indefinite possibilities of action. Thus Alexander of Abunoteichos not only succeeded in inventing a lucrative new worship of the serpent, but in getting adherents in various provinces. When every conceivable product of religious imagination is considered as in some way an expression of the supernatural and therefore to some extent valid, there remains no criterion in the light of which men can make up their minds about truth and error.

A certain semblance of order is, however, provided by the process of assimilating gods from one region with more or less comparable gods from another region. This process is called *interpretatio graeca* or *latina*. We are accustomed to the Graeco-Latin combinations. When we use them and speak of the identity of Ceres and Demeter we are apt to overlook the fact that such combinations are themselves forms of syncretism. For the two partners of the combination have very different origins. Now the assimilation of more or less similar gods went exceedingly far and included more and more different religions. Thus we get groups or series in which we find gods of Greek, Roman, Syrian, Egyptian and Celtic background.[13] This process reaches its climax in the famous novel of Apuleius about the conversion of Lucius. Here it is said of Isis that she is the highest of all gods, the uniform face of the gods and goddesses whose unique divinity is worshipped in many different

---

[12] K. Latte, *op. cit.*, p. 44.
[13] Cf. P. Wendland, *Hellenistisch-Römische Kultur*, 2nd ed., 1912, p. 131.

ways and rites and under many various names by the whole world (*cuius numen unicum multiformi specie, ritu vario, nomine multiiugo totus veneratur orbis*). There follows a list of these other names: the Great Mother, Minerva, Venus, Diana, Proserpina, Ceres, Juno, Bellona, Hecate, Rhamnusia.[14]

The quotation is especially interesting in that it shows how the tendency to unify the gods must lead inevitably to a type of monotheism in which all gods become different forms of one and the same reality. This tendency was strongly supported by the philosophers. All worship has finally to do with the same deity who is worshipped under different names. It is this philosophical blend of monotheism and polytheism which inspired the Emperor Julian in his attempt to resuscitate paganism over against Christianity. The later Neo-platonic philosophers had taught him that all myths could be interpreted symbolically, and so Julian dreamt of a sort of pagan church which would embrace all cults—except of course the Christian faith, which refused such religious co-existence. In fact, the pantheon of Julian looked, as one of his latest biographers remarks, rather like a museum of theological antiquities.[15]

The case of the Emperor Julian reminds us of the curious relation between politics and syncretism. Already in the beginning of our period we find Ptolemy I, the first Greek king of Egypt, creating the cult of Sarapis in order to bring Egyptian and Greek religion closer together and so to provide (what would be called to-day) an unifying ideology for his state. His two advisers were the Egyptian priest Manetho and the Eleusinian priest Timotheus. The astonishing thing is that this god, constructed for specifically political reasons, became a great success. He was combined with Pluto,

[14] N. Turchi, *Fontes Historiae Mysteriorum*, Rome, 1923, p. 195. Cf. A. D. Nock, *Conversion*, p. 150. See also Oxyrhynchus Pap. 1380, quoted by Turchi, p. 179.
[15] Cf. J. Bidez, *La vie de l'empereur Julien*, 1930, pp. 252ff.

Dionysus, Helios and even with Zeus. Some four centuries after he had been conceived we find him in a strong position in Rome, where he becomes 'pantheos', a universal and inclusive god acclaimed with the words: 'There is only one Zeus-Sarapis.'[16]

In a similar way the cult of the Sun-god, of which the Emperor Aurelian was the chief promoter, was intended to unify the empire on the basis of: one god, one empire, one emperor.[17] The origin of this sun-worship was Syria (Emesa), but many other religious movements, especially Mithraism, had paved the way for a solar pantheism.[18] So the prospects for the *Sol Invictus* seemed bright. But we are now at the end of the third century. The Christian God, who was not a product of philosophical speculation or political calculation, was winning the hearts of men. The date of our Christmas, chosen so as to set the birth of Christ over against the festival of birth of the *Sol Invictus* on December 25, reminds us of one of the last great attempts to create a syncretistic imperial religion.

The most nearly successful attempts to give the ancient world one common faith did however come from an unexpected quarter, namely from Persia. Twice during our period religious systems which built syncretistic structures on a basis of old Persian religious insights made a bid for the spiritual supremacy of the ancient world. These were Mithraism and Manicheism. Both, says the great specialist on this subject, Franz Cumont, 'had been formed in the Orient from a mixture of the ancient Babylonian mythology with Persian dualism and had afterwards absorbed Hellenic elements'.[19]

[16] F. Cumont, *Oriental Religions*, pp. 74f. and 84; A. D. Nock, *Conversion*, p. 38.

[17] H. Lietzmann, *From Constantine to Julian* (History of the Early Church III), ET, 1950, p. 20.

[18] Franz Altheim, *Der unbesiegte Gott*, 1957, p. 95.

[19] F. Cumont, *The Mysteries of Mithra*, p. 207.

Mithraism had its period of widespread influence from the first to the fourth century of our era. With its emphasis on courage, truthfulness and solidarity it was above all a religion for soldiers and found therefore favour in imperial circles. Its appeal was comprehensive in that it offered at the same time a doctrine of salvation, an initiation to the higher life, an ethic, a cosmology and an eschatology. Again it was a hospitable religion which made place for other gods and myths. Thus it could appeal to the educated as well as the simple-minded.[20] 'Mithraism, at least in the fourth century, had therefore as its end aim the union of all gods and mysteries in a vast synthesis—the foundation of a new religion in harmony with the prevailing philosophy and political constitution of the empire.'[21] There was a time when it seemed that Mithraism was the world religion of the future. Why then did it fail? Was it not because it sought to embrace so much, that it became inherently contradictory? Cumont shows that while there are many points of resemblance between Mithraism and Christianity one great difference lies in their attitude to paganism.[22] Mithraism made its peace with all the various forms of nature-religion. Christianity made its prophetic protest against all forms of worship of the created world. The more consistent religion proved to be stronger.

But even before Mithraism lost its influence a second religion with Persian credentials came upon the scene. Mani founded his new religion in the middle of the third century. Less than fifty years later it had already become sufficiently powerful to make it necessary for Emperor Diocletian to issue an order to suppress it. But it continued to advance. We know from the *Confessions* of St Augustine what influence it exerted in Africa, but it became equally powerful in the West and spread even to China. Mani's purpose was to create a religion which would not be linked with any

---

[20] *Ibid.*, p. 148.   [21] *Ibid.*, p. 187.   [22] F. Cumont, *op. cit.*, p. 197.

one nation or culture but be definitely universal from the very outset. He considered his church as superior to all previous ones, in that it was a church for the whole world.[23] Now his universalism consisted (as in so many later syncretisms) in declaring that all previous revelations had only provisional and relative validity, but that his revelation, in which the former ones were included, was the final and absolute divine truth. Thus Buddha, Zoroaster and Jesus are recognized as forerunners. But it is typical that Jesus is understood as one of the persons of the mythical drama who proclaims the divine nature of the imprisoned souls of men and not as the Saviour who has entered into history and died on the cross for man's salvation. The basic purpose of this system is totally different from the purpose of Christianity. Its absolute dualism leads to a denial of the Creator God and to a form of otherworldliness which is really a rejection of life in this world.

With Manicheism we have already entered into the strange and complicated world of the many gnostic systems. At this point we need only note that gnosticism, however Christian it may seem to be in some of its forms, is essentially a form of syncretism. In such documents as those of the Naassenes[24] in which the myth of Attis (who is also Adonis, Osiris, etc.) is interpreted as identical with the Christian gospel or, conversely, Jesus is set in the framework of the typically gnostic doctrine concerning release of the divine spark in men, the syncretism is obvious. Here Jesus says: 'I will show the form of the gods; and I will deliver under the name of gnosis the secrets of the holy way.' But even where the language and thought forms seem to be much more closely related to those of the New Testament the structure of thought in gnostic writings is non-

[23] H. Lietzmann, *The Founding of the Church Universal* (History of the Early Church II), ET, 3rd ed., 1953, p. 270.
[24] *Gnosticism: An Anthology*, ed. Robert M. Grant, 1961, p. 105.

21

biblical and betrays its non-Christian origin. Where esoteric knowledge is the central category there is no place for the unique historical revelation, no place for the incarnation. And to combine such gnosis with Christianity is to create a hybrid religion. We will have to come back to this in our next chapter.

At the very end of this period the Roman prefect Symmachus summarized in his protest to the Emperor the basic concept underlying the whole syncretistic movement. 'What does it matter how anyone seeks the truth? It is impossible that so great a mystery should be approached by one road only.'[25] These words, *'uno itinere non potest perveniri ad tam grande secretum'*, represent the challenge of syncretism to Christianity. This challenge was inadequately met by the official suppression of pagan cults. It could only be dealt with as a spiritual problem, and the Christian Church would have to confront it again and again.

The third wave of syncretism

The third great syncretistic wave is that which broke over Europe in the eighteenth century. It had been prepared by the Renaissance and the Enlightenment. But these two forces had been too sterile in the realm of religion to produce a forceful syncretism. They had however succeeded in shaking the foundations of the all too secure and static ecclesiastical orthodoxy. They had revolted against the uniqueness which the Church had claimed for the history of salvation. They had discovered the astounding multiplicity of religious possibilities. They had looked for the common factor in all religions, and in the eighteenth century they found this in the three concepts of God, Virtue and Immortality. But this thin remnant of religion could hardly be expected to take the place of the Christian faith.

The significance of Rousseau is that he made natural re-

[25] Gaston Boissier, *La Fin du Paganisme* II, p. 278.

ligion a serious competitor to revealed religion. The natural religion of the deists and sceptics had in fact been an attack on all religion. Rousseau showed that it was possible to have a religion which would in no way depart from the basic immanentist and anthropocentric assumptions of the Enlightenment, but still meet the deep human need for adoration and worship. His natural religion contains that 'enthusiasm' which Madame de Stael found wanting in the French thinkers and which she discovered in Germany. And Joubert was therefore right when he said that Voltaire's irreligion was in the long run less dangerous for religiously sensitive people than the pseudo-religion of Rousseau.[26] Rousseau's basic principle is that 'le culte essentiel est celui du coeur' (the essential cult is that of the heart).[27] The religion which after closing all other books and reading only the book of nature I discover in my own heart and conscience is wholly adequate and gives me all I need. 'What moral purity, what dogma useful to men can I draw from any positive (that is historical) doctrine, which I cannot learn without such doctrine by the good use of my faculties?'[28] Revelation in historical events is not only superfluous. It degrades God; it makes him appear unjust in that he is supposed to produce as his credentials some particular signs done among obscure people.[29] It makes men intolerant. A God who begins by choosing one people alone is not the common father of all men. On the other hand natural religion is truly universal. 'If men had only listened to what God says in their hearts, there would never have been more than one religion in the world.'[30] Nevertheless the particular historical religions have a certain function. They are all good if in them men serve God decently. Their

[26] Quoted by Irving Babbitt, *Masters of modern French Criticism*, 1912, p. 41.
[27] *Emile* (Classiques Garnier), p. 381. All following quotations are from the 'Profession de Foi du Vicaire Savoyard'.
[28] *Op. cit.*, p. 361.   [29] *Op. cit.*, p. 363.   [30] *Op. cit.*, p. 361.

differences have only to do with climate, government, national character. God does not reject a worship which comes from the heart and is sincere, in whatever form it may be offered to him.[31]

Thus Rousseau opened the door for that new and truly human religion without revelation which made it possible to embrace at one and the same time all religious experiences and discoveries of mankind without excluding any.

No one has taken greater advantage of that situation than Goethe. His works contain of course the most diverse and contradictory statements about his religious attitude. Thus it is possible to find in them not only expressions of a real hatred of Christianity but also of admiration for Christ. But there is little variation in the main theme of this symphony. That theme is syncretism. It is not the arid, rationalistic deduction of some unsubstantial common denominator, but rather the eager reception of all the wealth of varieties of religious experience of mankind, in other words a specifically religious syncretism.

Goethe, like Rousseau, seeks the universal, fully inclusive religion which can become the religion of mankind as a whole. In his poem 'Die Geheimnisse' the central figure who embodies the highest common insights that men have attained is called 'Humanus'. For religion is in his view basically a human affair. God is essentially unknowable.[32] At the end of his pilgrimage Faust confesses that the view towards the world above is not given to man, just as the younger Faust had already said to Gretchen: 'Who can name him?' Is there then no revelation? Not in the sense of a unique self-communication of God in history. 'The seeker does not let himself be robbed of the heritage given to the whole world',[33] and therefore no one must call his faith the

[31] *Op. cit.*, p. 381.
[32] 'In jenes Namen der so oft genannt
   Dem Wesen nach blieb immer unbekannt.' *Gott und Welt*, 1816.
[33] *Zahme Xenien*.

only one. When Lavater speaks of Christ as the one Saviour, Goethe answers that 'it is unjust and a robbery to pick up all the wonderful feathers of the thousand kinds of birds under heaven to decorate your bird of paradise'.[34] Revelation is to be found everywhere: in nature, in the Hellenic world, in ancient Oriental wisdom. In a letter to Jacobi (1813)[35] Goethe says: 'In view of the manifold tendencies of my nature one type of thinking is not enough for me. As poet and artist I am a polytheist, as a natural scientist I am a pantheist. . . . If I need a god for my personality as a moral being this is also taken care of.' Thus Goethe's religious world is of bewildering variety. Faust begins and ends with scenes set in a classical Christian framework, but in between we find that the dominating forces, such as the spirit of the earth, the mothers, Helena or the demonic powers of the two Walpurgis-nights, have their origin in non-Christian religions. Except for a certain period when Goethe wrote specifically anti-Christian poems, such as the one about the Diana of the Ephesians, Christianity becomes in his mind simply one element of the wider religious synthesis.

This becomes especially clear in the later years. In 'Wilhelm Meister's Wanderjahre' Christianity is described as one of three religions which together produce the one true religion.[36] In 1831 Goethe rejoices in the discovery of the strange sect of Hypsistarians, one of the syncretistic sects in the Roman Empire, which he describes as a sect wedged in between pagans, Jews and Christians. He adds: 'I felt that during my whole life I had tried to qualify as a Hypsistarian.'[37] So we are not astonished to hear his last words on religion spoken on March 11, 1832, eleven days

---

[34] In a letter dated June 22, 1781.
[35] K. Sell, *Die Religion unserer Klassiker*, 1904, p. 168.
[36] Book II. 1.
[37] K. Sell, *op. cit.*, p. 165.

before his death, and which Eckermann has recorded.[38] Goethe says first of all that there is an *'Urreligion'*, a basic religion, that of pure nature and reason, and that this is of divine origin. The standpoint of the Church is more human and mediates the pure unspoiled revelation to weak men. Does Goethe believe in Christ? 'Yes,' says he, 'I bow down before him as the divine revelation of the highest principle of morality. But if you ask me whether it is my nature to pay honour to the Sun, I say again: Certainly, for it is equally a revelation of the highest and the most powerful which we children of the earth are allowed to observe.'

Goethe's syncretism is so deeply impressive because it seems to be a successful synthesis of all religious strivings of men. That is why he has found so many followers, not only in Germany, but in Britain where Carlyle became his prophet, in America where Emerson praised him, in France where Madame de Stael introduced him. But was the synthesis truly successful? Or had it only succeeded because Goethe had refused to ask the deeper questions about the meaning of each of the religions concerned? In fact was it a real synthesis or did not *Faust*, especially in its second part with its unresolved conflicts between Christian and pagan motifs, between grace and works, between this-worldly and other-worldly forces, between God and Mephisto, show that he had produced a religious museum rather than a coherent world-view? It is true that Goethe was a poet and should not be judged as a theologian, but when poets speak as prophets should they not lead us to the fundamental truths?

In any case another poet who lived at that same time and struggled with the same vital issues has demonstrated that a serious attempt to combine the religion of nature with the revelation in Christ is more likely to end in tragedy. I refer to Hölderlin, perhaps the greatest of all German poets,

[38] Eckermann, *Gespräche mit Goethe*, Munich, 1949, pp. 408f.

26

whose life and poetry are dominated by the attempt to hold together the religion of Hellas and the Christian faith. We shall never know how far this fundamental conflict contributed to the disastrous crisis, when the poet lost his mind. He had begun by studying theology, but before long he became fascinated by ancient Greece. In this case it was not merely an aesthetic enthusiasm. He actually became a Greek in his religion. No other Western poet in modern history has identified himself so deeply with the Greek religion of nature, of the cosmic powers, of the many divinities which are finally all manifestations of the same rhythmic movement of life and death. His great complaint is that these gods have left us and that thus the world has become lifeless and grey. But he cannot forget the other God whom he has known before. So he must confront the ancient question : what has Christ to do with the old gods? The most revealing and moving answer to this decisive question is given in 'Der Einzige' ('The Unique'). The poem begins with another evocation of the Greek world. 'I *am* there, where Apollo went in his royal stature.' But moving among the ancient gods the poet seeks still another one whom he loves. This is his master and lord, Christ. Do the gods really claim that if he serves this lord all the rest, all the glory of the ancient pantheon will be lost to him? No, Christ is the brother of Heracles and the brother of Dionysus. These three have the same father. These three are similar to each other ('So sind jene sich gleich'). The world is one and the same world in which everything is related to everything else.

Thus the unique one is not unique in that he stands apart; he is unique only in that he is one of the true expressions of the oneness that lies behind all appearance.

It is clear that we have here a syncretism which does not arise out of a lack of understanding of the gulf between the pagan and the Christian faith, but rather out of a desperate desire to hold on to two different faiths which are known to be profoundly dissimilar, but both of which are too precious to be abandoned. It is not without significance that in our day there has been a veritable Hölderlin-renaissance. Modern man recognizes in him not only the incomparable poet, but also the representative of that 'secret religion of the intellectuals' which is a nostalgic groping for the manifold treasures of religious life through the ages, but which does not lead to any higher certainty than that of the existence of an elusive and impenetrable mystery clothing itself in endless forms.

The fourth wave of syncretism

The fourth wave of syncretism is that with which we are confronted to-day. Is it really a fourth wave, or is it simply the continuation of the third one? Although syncretism has flourished in various schools of thought during the whole period since the days of Rousseau and Goethe I speak of a new wave because of the new factors which have begun to operate more recently.

These factors are especially the following. As a specific science comparative religion is quite young and dates from the middle of the nineteenth century. Its results, which have become increasingly popularized (see the stream of pocket-books on the subject), have inevitably led to a questioning of the uniqueness of Christian faith, and this all the more so since it seemed to be possible to explain practically every aspect of the Christian faith in terms of concepts and myths which were equally to be found in other religions. This view was reinforced by the new schools of psychology which presented differences in faith as varieties of religious experience and often went on to evaluate religious convictions not in terms of truth and error, but in terms of their functional value for the self-realization of the individual. At the same time the position of Christianity as the religion of the strong and powerful nations was greatly weakened as we came to the end of what Dr Panikkar has called 'the age of Vasco da Gama', that is the age of Western domination. The old religions of Asia, about which Western observers had too easily prophesied that they were slowly dying out, show remarkable vitality and develop increasingly a missionary consciousness. Through various channels, Eastern missionary organizations, syncretistic movements, modern philosophical and literary trends, Eastern religious thought penetrates the West as Western thought has penetrated the East. The *raison d'être* of Christian missions is questioned by large circles in Europe and America as well as in Asia. In the vitalist philosophy which is so marked a feature of our modern literature, there is a revolt against the Jewish prophetic and Christian tradition and a nostalgia for the ancient religions of nature. And there is finally the widespread conviction that in a time when the world has politically and technically become one world it is imperative to find an universal religion which will unite men into one worshipping community and provide the greatly needed common ethos for international relations.

Now modern syncretism is such a complex phenomenon that we cannot possibly describe it here in all its many forms. We will therefore have to choose some typical examples in various realms of life and thought. Thus we will use illustrations from the domains of literature, of psychology, of the philosophy of history, all in the Western world, then turn to some of the main forms of syncretism in Asia and finally deal with the international movements and sects which proclaim the harmony of all religions.

In the field of literature syncretism has been going strong for a long time. In Walt Whitman's *Leaves of Grass* of 1867 America is addressed in these terms:

'Thee in thy all-supplying all-enclosing worship—
   thee in no single bible, saviour, merely,

Thy saviours countless, latent within thyself,
   thy bibles incessant within thyself, equal to any,
                    divine as any . . .'

But perhaps the most influential voice was that of D. H. Lawrence. Can we then call him a syncretist? In many of his works he defends a really purely pagan religion of total adjustment to the deep vital forces of nature. He calls men out of the bourgeois civilization which suppresses life, and wants them to rediscover 'the recklessness of Pan; trusting deep down to the springs of nature'.[39] It is therefore rather surprising that the great debate about *Lady Chatterley's Lover* has taken the form of a debate as to its morality or immorality. It is not an immoral but a thoroughly pagan book, with a pagan morality. Lawrence desired to proclaim a new faith. He calls his book 'frankly and faithfully a phallic novel'[40] in other words a novel that seeks to resuscitate the spirit of the ancient fertility cults. But this very inability of our contemporaries to recognize paganism when they see it, is a clear indication of the syncretistic atmosphere in which we live to-day. And Lawrence has made a contribution to syncretism which is far more shocking than any straightforwardly pagan novel can be. This is his sacrilegious story *The Man who Died*, in which the risen Christ discovers true life when he embraces the priestess of the temple of Isis. For what is more profoundly profane than this distortion of all that we know of Christ: 'He said: "This is the great atonement, the being in touch. The grey sea and the rain, the wet narcissus and the woman I wait for, the invisible Isis and the unseen sun are all in touch and at one." '[41] Neither the ancient nor the modern Oriental world have ever produced a piece of syncretism

[39] In a letter of 1924, quoted by Mabel Dodge Luhan, *Lorenzo in Taos*, 1933, p. 129.
[40] In a letter of 1928, quoted *ibid.*, p. 305.
[41] *The Man who Died*, Tauchnitz, 1932, p. 66.

that is so utterly lacking in reverence for the Christian Gospel or for religious truth in general.

Our next illustration is in the field of psychology. In that realm the most powerful force making for a syncretistic mood is the school of which Carl Gustav Jung is the founder. Its significance lies in the fact that it takes religion seriously as an indispensable factor in the life of individuals and civilizations. Jung believes that the soul of man is *'naturaliter religiosa'*.[42] Man can try to suppress it, but it will only take refuge in the realm of unconsciousness. It is a question of to be or not to be for us, whether we succeed in finding a readjustment to this great realm.[43] In it are contained the treasures of the collective religious experiences of mankind which reappear as archetypes in our dreams. Now there can be no doubt that by this new approach Jung has opened up new perspectives for psychotherapy as well as for the study of religions. He has a perfect right to do what he says he wants to do, namely to analyse objectively the psychological phenomena of a religious character and to include the phenomena of Christian religious life in his field of study. But he is in fact not content with analysis alone. One of his admirers has rightly said that Jung has transformed psychoanalysis into psychosynthesis.[44] In spite of his own protestations that he is only an objective scientist we find him constantly taking the role of the prophet who establishes norms of religious life and makes value-judgments concerning specific forms of religion.[45]

Jung warns against a cheap syncretism. He does not believe that Europeans who with respect to religious symbols have become beggars, should try to hide their nakedness

[42] *Bewusstes und Unbewusstes*, Fischer Bücherei, p. 64.
[43] *Ibid.*, p. 33.
[44] S. Vestdijk, *De Toekomst der Religie*, 1947, p. 350.
[45] See in *Bewusstes und Unbewusstes* the contrast between pp. 65 and 67.

with beautiful Oriental robes.[46] But he states at the same time that the basic religious experiences in the various religions mean one and the same thing. When St Paul says that it is no longer he that lives but Christ that lives in him, this is the same psychological event which Lao Tse describes as Tao.[47] Christianity is just one of the mystery religions.[48] It is to be regretted that our civilization does not know the healing experiences which the Eleusinian mysteries provided in their time.[49]

So we are prepared for the question: 'Is it not conceivable that one could take the decision not to act as *arbiter mundi* . . . and to hold the faith, that God has expressed himself in many languages and in manifold phenomena and that all these statements are *true*?'[50]

We are inclined to answer by another question: Is it not possible that by making the choice for this ancient relativism and religious pluralism the psychologist is in fact setting himself up as the final arbiter? One of his followers has already suggested that governments should accept responsibility for religious education to be given on the basis of Jung's psychology.[51] In any case the Jung psychology has directly or indirectly the effect of creating a religious eclecticism in which the most divergent religious concepts are collected without any real spiritual discrimination.[52]

In the field of the philosophy of history we find of course a very strong concern about the lack of a unifying religion

[46] *Ibid.*, p. 23.
[47] 'The Relation between the Ego and the Unconscious' in *Two Essays on Analytical Psychology*, ET, 1953, p. 220.
[48] *Ibid.*, p. 233.
[49] *Introduction to a Science of Mythology*, ET, 1951, p. 226.
[50] *Bewusstes und Unbewusstes*, p. 66 (Jung's italics).
[51] S. Vestdijk, *De Toekomst der Religie*, p. 351.
[52] See the sourcebook *The Choice is always Ours*, by D. B. Phillips and others, 1960, a specific example of modern syncretism with more extracts from the works of Jung than from anyone else.

at a time when political, economic and technical factors force mankind to live as one coherent unit. Thus Professor Northrop of Yale has sought to make a philosophical analysis of the ingredients of the various civilizations in order to see in which way these ingredients can be harmoniously combined into an integrated whole. With regard to religion his conclusion is that, in order to reach that harmony, 'determinate moral and religious commandments or theses arrived at by nomadic tribes in the Mediterranean region in the time of Moses or the time of Christ simply cannot be taken as perfect and sufficient determinate theses for the definition of the good life in the twentieth century, even in the West, to say nothing of the Orient'.[53] A new theistic theology is to be constructed. Elements of that theology must be 'the intuitive and contemplative, indeterminate, aesthetic and emotional religion of the Orient, the negative theology of the West, the mysticism of San Juan de la Cruz, and the cult of the Virgin at Chartres, and Guadelupe; rather than the theoretical, doctrinal orthodox religion of the male Moses, Christ or Mohammed and their determinate unseen Yahveh or God the Father'.[54] After hearing this we are not surprised to be told that 'Western religious leaders with an adequate idea of the good and the divine will go to the East more to acquire its religion of intuition and contemplation than to convert the Easterner to the Western theistic religion of doctrine and reform'.[55] This is a thorough syncretism, but it has at least this advantage that it clearly recognizes that in this philosophically constructed religion Christianity must be left out as being too 'determinate', that is, as having a specific historical revelation at its centre.

Professor W. E. Hocking has a more profound view of religion and a deeper understanding of history. He gives us

[53] F. S. C. Northrop, *The Meeting of East and West*, 1946, p. 460.
[54] *Ibid.*, p. 462.   [55] *Ibid.*, p. 455.

B   33

a searching analysis of the predicament of the modern
world in which the 'abstract universals' have the great
penetrating power, but the 'concrete universals', of which
religion is one, do not progress with the same speed. Can
Christianity become truly universal? The essence of Christianity is discussed. Its faith-content is described thus:
'The nature of things is divine love for the created world, a
love that suffers.'[56] At this point we begin to wonder. Can
the Christian faith be defined without reference to the facts
of the birth, life, death and resurrection of Jesus Christ?
Professor Hocking admits that every religion must be historical to be effective, but, as Bishop Newbigin has pointed
out, he does not seem to realize that in the case of Christianity this must apply especially 'to the historic events
which are the objects of the Church's faith'.[57] It is because
Professor Hocking does not include them that he can come
to the conclusion that the several universal religions are
already fused together, so to speak, at the top.[58] Yes, if
Christianity can dispense with the deeds of God, the events
of the history of salvation, then it is possible to arrive at a
synthesis on the basis of a timeless mysticism. And then it
is conceivable that, as Professor Hocking thinks, it will
become part of a world-religion which may or may not use
the name of Christ, but which will represent an extension
of the concept of the Christ to include that unbound Spirit
who stands and has stood at the door of every man. But in
that case we are no longer concerned with the real Jesus
whom we find in the New Testament. We are only left
with a Christ-concept vaguely related to the historical
record.

Professor Arnold Toynbee believes also that the time has
come for a *rapprochement* of the religions. He agrees with

[56] W. E. Hocking, *The Coming World Civilisation*, 1956, p. 108.
[57] Lesslie Newbigin, *A Faith for this one World?*, 1961, p. 51.
[58] *Op. cit.*, p. 149.

Symmachus, the defender of the old Roman religion, that it is unthinkable that 'so great a mystery should be approached by one road only'. He has recently declared war on all who in any way believe in a chosen people and a unique truth. He rejects definitely what he calls the 'argument' of the Christian Church that it is unique in virtue of the uniqueness of Christ and of his incarnation. It is not credible that 'God who is another name for love and who is believed to have demonstrated his love for Man by becoming incarnate in a human being, will have done this self-sacrificing deed of emptying himself at one time and place and one only'.[59] What remains are the teachings of Christianity. But these are not exclusively Christian. For the idea of God's self-sacrifice is found in ancient nature-worship and in Buddhism. We must expect that the religions will become increasingly ready to learn from each other. Professor Toynbee does not think that an artificially syncretistic religion will emerge, but having seen the Bahai temple near Chicago he nevertheless wonders whether this beautiful building is not a portent of the future.[60] It is remarkable to find that Professor Toynbee, exactly as Professors Northrop and Hocking, discusses Christianity wholly in terms of ideas. But Christianity is not a philosophical system; it is, as Bishop Newbigin says, 'primarily news and only secondarily views'.[61] And if the news is denied, the views hang in the air.

Eastern syncretism

We must now turn to the syncretistic movements in the East. We deliberately deal with them after those of the West so as to counteract the mistaken notion that syncretism is a specifically Eastern phenomenon. Though we

[59] In *The Observer*, April 16, 1961.
[60] *Christianity among the Religions of the World*, 1957, pp. 103-12.
[61] *A Faith for this one World?*, p. 45.

want to speak especially of recent developments, we must take note of one of the most grandiose syncretistic undertakings that has ever been made and the originator of which was not a Hindu, but a Moslem, namely Akbar the Great. He had tried to get the different religions to come to agreement and had failed. So he decided to create himself a new universal religion. He put his plan in these words: 'We ought therefore to bring them [the religions] into one, but in such a fashion that they should be both one and all; with the great advantage of not losing what is good in one religion, while gaining whatever is better in another. In that way, honour would be rendered to God, peace would be given to the peoples, and security to the Empire.'[62] So here we have a man of action who carries out with the full authority of the state the dream that so many have dreamt before and after him. The attempt failed altogether. The Jesuit historian whose account is based on the eye-witness of his colleagues at Akbar's Court remarks that one of the difficulties was that no one knew exactly which God they were henceforth supposed to adore. Akbar, who was certainly quite serious about the matter, had to learn that even an emperor cannot deal with religions as he deals with newly conquered provinces.

In the nineteenth century, however, there arose in India various movements which taught the essential harmony of the religions and which met with considerable success. The key figure is the great Hindu mystic Ramakrishna Paramahamsa, who left a very deep impression on all who came in contact with him. He was not a systematic teacher, but passed on his insights in the form of simple conversation or stories. According to one of his most loyal disciples 'he would speak of himself as the same soul that had been born before as Rama, as Krishna, as Jesus, or as Buddha, born

[62] Laurence Binyon, *Akbar*, 1932, p. 130. Cf. Daniello Bartoli, *La Mission al Gran Magor*, 1945 (reprint of the edition of 1653).

36

again as Ramakrishna'.[63] He taught not only that 'other religions also are paths leading to truth',[64] but he declared that he had actually practised all religions: Hinduism, Islam, Christianity, and that man instead of quarrelling should realize that he who is called Krishna is also called Shiva, Primitive Energy, Jesus or Allah.[65] This was not a rationalistic reduction of all religions to simple principles; this was a complete mystic identification with all forms of religious life. But it remained wholly conditioned by the Hindu conception of the inseparable unity between man and God. Ramakrishna is said to have inspired Keshab Chandra Sen to emphasize that all religions are true. In fact an extra-ordinary painting (reproduced in the volume of Farquhar) shows Ramakrishna teaching Keshab the harmony of all religions. The background is formed by a Hindu temple, a mosque and a church. In the forefront Christ performs a religious dance together with the Bengali sannyasi Chaitanya. Muslim, Sikh, Parsee, Confucian and Anglican clergy stand round them each carrying some symbol of their various faiths.

But the man who made Ramakrishna's teachings known all over India and indeed in the whole world is Swami Vivekenanda. Through his journeys to the West and especially his participation in the World's Parliament of Religions in Chicago in 1893, through the creation of the Ramakrishna Mission with its world-wide programme and through capturing the allegiance of the great French author Romain Rolland, Vivekenanda became the foremost exponent of the 'Universal Gospel' with its basic tenet that there is a fundamental harmony between all religions. Vivekenanda accepts all religions, old and new, and worships God with all of

[63] Vivekenanda, quoted by J. N. Farquhar, *Modern Religious Movements in India*, 1915, p. 195.
[64] *Ibid.*, p. 198.
[65] Romain Rolland, *Prophets of the New India*, ET, 1930, p. 56.

them.[66] At the Parliament of Religions in Chicago he appealed to his hearers to proclaim to the world that the Lord is in every religion and exclaimed: 'May he who is the Brahma of the Hindus, the Ahura Mazda of the Zoroastrians, the Buddha of the Buddhists, the Jehovah of the Jews, the Father in Heaven of the Christians give strength to you to carry out your noble idea.'[67] All paths lead to the same God. If therefore 'anybody dreams of the exclusive survival of his own (religion) and the destruction of the others, I pity him from the bottom of my heart'.[68] That his appeal was not unsuccessful is shown by the comment of the *New York Herald*: 'Vivekenanda is undoubtedly the greatest figure in the Parliament of Religions. After hearing him we feel how foolish it is to send missionaries to this learned nation [i.e. India].'[69]

But what is this harmony of all religions which Vivekenanda presents? Is it a real synthesis in which the fundamental convictions of each are taken fully seriously? It seems to me that the answer to that question is contained in one of Vivekenanda's letters. He says: 'Whether we call it Vedantism or any *ism*, the truth is that Advaitism [i.e. the monism in which God and the self are identical] is the last word of religion and the only position from which one can look upon all religions and sects with love. We believe it is the religion of the future enlightened humanity.'[70] It is remarkable that thus there is one religion, in fact *only* one religion which is to gather up all religion and thus in fact to supplant them. Are we not thus far away from the Chicago plea that henceforth there should be peaceful co-

[66] Romain Rolland, *Prophets of the New India*, p. 444.

[67] *Neely's History of the Parliament of Religions*, by W. R. Houghton, 1894. p. 445.

[68] *Ibid.*, p. 853.

[69] Quoted by Farquhar, *op. cit.*, p. 202.

[70] Quoted by Jawaharlal Nehru, *The Discovery of India*, 3rd ed., 1951, p. 317. The letter is dated 1898.

existence between the religions? And does this not mean that while all religions are equal, the Vedanta religion is more equal than the others?

The religious thought of Mahatma Gandhi is essentially in line with that of Ramakrishna and Vivekenanda. He also taught that the religions represent different roads which lead to one and the same goal. To Dr John R. Mott, who asked him whether he disbelieved in all conversion, Gandhi said: 'My effort should never be to undermine another's faith, but to make him a better follower of his own faith. This implies belief in the truth of all religions and, therefore, respect for them.'[71] Gandhi had been deeply impressed by the New Testament to which, according to his own admission, he owed his insight concerning the power of nonviolent resistance. He spoke of Christ as a radiant revelation of God. But he added that he did not put him on the throne alone.[72] Similarly he said in 1928: 'After long study and experience I have come to these conclusions that (1) all religions are true, (2) all religions have some error in them, (3) all religions are almost as dear to me as my own Hinduism. My veneration for other faiths is the same as for my own faith. Consequently the thought of conversion is impossible.'[73]

The most influential Eastern spokesman for the harmonizing of religions is to-day Dr Radhakrishnan, philosopher as well as statesman. In his writings the Hindu concept of the fundamental unity of all religions is worked out in a much more precise manner and in the categories of modern thought. There can be no doubt that Dr Radhakrishnan offers us a real syncretism. His hope is that 'Muslim and Christian, Buddhist and Hindu shall stand together bound by a common devotion . . . to a great dream of a world

---

[71] *The Student World*, October 1929.
[72] Romain Rolland, *Mahatma Gandhi*, ET, 1924, p. 31.
[73] Quoted in Nehru, *The Discovery of India*, p. 340.

society with a universal religion of which the historical faiths are but branches'.[74] But this syncretism is not really inclusive and not truly universal. For it is made abundantly clear that what Dr Radhakrishnan calls the 'orthodoxies' can have no place in it. The ambiguity of the approach is already apparent in the preface of *Eastern Religions and Western Thought*. For we read there on the one hand that 'the supreme task of our generation is to give a soul to the growing world-consciousness',[75] but we are told also that 'while the different religions in their historical forms bind us to limited groups and militate against the development of loyalty to a world-community, the mystics have always stood for the fellowship of humanity'.[76] We are invited to work toward the 'larger synthesis' of 'believers with different opinions',[77] but we find that the nature of the synthesis is already predetermined, for the one and only possible synthesis is that on the basis of the mystic tradition which has its real origin in India, but which exists everywhere. These mystics 'belong to a movement that is worldwide; their temple is not the chapel of a sect, but a vast pantheon'.[78] In other words we are all urged to enter this particular pantheon and to leave our so-called historical religions behind.

This form of syncretism has therefore a fighting character. The theologies of Barth and Brunner are declared to be narrow orthodoxies the weakness of which is spiritual cowardice.[79] The position of the Confessing Church in Germany and the national socialist ideology are described as a common reaction against liberalism.[80] What is really wrong with historical Christianity is its dependence on the Jewish inheritance, because the Jews considered it to be the great sin to desert their own true God, and go after others.[81] So

[74] *Eastern Religions and Western Thought*, 2nd ed., 1940, p. 347.
[75] *Op. cit.*, p. viii.   [76] *Op. cit.*, p. ix.   [77] *Op. cit.*, p. 348.
[78] *Op. cit.*, p. 296.   [79] *Op. cit.*, p. 285.   [80] *Op. cit.*, p. 286.
[81] *Op. cit.*, p. 331.

this universalism is in fact a call to the mystics of the world to unite against those who believe in specific revelation in history. It is highly doubtful whether such a call is really a contribution to the unification of humanity.

Syncretistic movements and sects

It is not surprising that the very general desire for a true universalism has in the syncretistic atmosphere of our time led to the formation of movements and sects which teach the essential oneness of all religions or seek to combine the main tenets of a number of historical religions. What is surprising is rather the large number of such bodies. If we only take those which have an international significance, we find that there are a considerable number which seek to establish a world-religion based on the claim that in their particular system the discord of the religions has been overcome and the true harmony of religions has been established.

What then are their differences? Why do they not harmonize their attempts at harmonization? One reason is that each gives a great and central place to its special prophet or founder. Another is that each has grown up in a particular religious soil and betrays in some way or another the nature of its origins. It is clearly almost impossible to create what might be called an absolute or wholly objective syncretism. In actual fact every syncretism is somebody's syncretism. The original structure of each religious faith is so strong that it continues to dominate the thought and expression even of those who decide to create a religion acceptable to all men everywhere.

Thus we have two influential syncretistic movements which have grown up in the soil of Hinduism. One is that of the Ramakrishna-Mission which proclaims the 'universal gospel' of Ramakrishna and Vivekenanda. We have already seen how deeply that gospel is coloured by the Advaita philosophy of non-dualism and the identity of God and man. The mission develops a world-wide activity. Its one objective has remained to establish harmony and co-operation among the beliefs and doctrines of the whole of humanity.[82] There is however another movement which has its basis in Hinduism. This is the Theosophical Society. This movement has had a strange history. Its founder, Madame Blavatsky, was an enigmatic personality. Her work *Isis unveiled*[83] is almost an encyclopaedia of gnostic and esoteric materials of all ages written in the form of a violent attack upon traditional Christian theology. Farquhar has told the astonishing story of her attempt to make the world believe that she was in touch with the Masters or Mahatmas in Tibet, who were the guardians of the ancient wisdom.[84] The society has, however, exerted considerable influence in the West. It teaches that 'there must be one truth which finds expression in all the various religions—except in the Jewish'.[85] The formula is revealing, for it shows that the synthesis which theosophy seeks excludes the theocentric faith of Israel and therefore also a Christianity which recognizes the inseparable link between the Old and the New Testament. Theosophy is presented as a rediscovery of the ancient wisdom-religion. The name is derived from the eclectic philosopher Ammonias Saccas in the third century AD whose aim was 'to reconcile all religions, sects and nations under a common system of ethics, based on eternal verities'.[86] In this system Jesus becomes an avatar, one of 'the incarnations of a divinity', 'one in a long list of outstanding spiritual Great Ones, the Fine Flowers of the human race, who have lived and taught and

[82] Romain Rolland, *Prophets of the New India*, p. 495.
[83] Original edition in 1877, reprinted in 1960.
[84] *Modern Religious Movements in India*, pp. 227ff.
[85] Madame Blavatsky, *The Key to Theosophy* (reprinted in 1946), p. 45.
[86] *Key to Theosophy*, p. 3.

42

ennobled their fellow-men'.[87] At the headquarters in Adhyar (India) one finds therefore statues of all great religious teachers.

Similarly two movements of universal faith have grown up in a Moslem environment. One is the Bahai world faith, which grew up in the nineteenth century in Iran, but which has now become a widespread international movement. It teaches that religious truth is not absolute, but relative, that the divine revelation is progressive, that all religions are divine in origin, that their fundamental principles are in harmony with each other and that they reflect one and the same truth. The nine doors through which one can enter the great Bahai temple in Wilmette near Chicago represent the nine religions of the world. But each religion has not only an eternal, but also a temporary, historically conditioned aspect. The greatness of Baha Ullah was that he purified all religions, so that in the Bahai faith they all find the essence of their religion and the definitive revelation. Baha Ullah has been the Messiah which in some manner all religions expected. Thus he could say: 'For whereas in days past every lover besought and searched after his Beloved, it is the Beloved Himself Who is now calling His lovers and is inviting them to attain His presence.'[88] The Bahai faith provides a basis for a re-ordering of the world in such a way that humanity shall live as one united family. Here as in other similar systems Jesus becomes one of the many religious prophets and one who was only a forerunner of Baha Ullah. The result of the forced synthesis is that only a pale common denominator of the religions is left.

Bahai is therefore a new composite religion which replaces the old religions. The other movement with a Moslem background does not offer a new religion, but simply pro-

---

[87] G. de Purucker, *Questions we all ask* III, 1948, p. 185.
[88] *The Glad Tidings of Baha' U'llah*, with Introduction and Notes by George Townshend, 1949, p. 60. See also p. 73.

claims that all historical religions are expressions of the one universal religion. As its name indicates, the movement is based on the mysticism of the medieval Sufis in Iran, though the modern Sufi-movement was created by Inayat Khan in the beginning of this century. Esoterically understood all religions speak of one and the same god. There is only one master who has appeared on earth in the form of Buddha, Jesus, Mohammed, Krishna, Confucius, Lao Tse and Inayat Khan himself. The seven candles in the worship service represent the seven religions, and lessons are read from the books of all of them. But here also we find that the formulation of the basic concept is: 'There is only one truth: the knowledge of our own nature: know yourself and you will know God.'[89] Or, as Inayat Khan said elsewhere: 'God is God and man is man, yet God is man and man is God.'[90] Thus this movement also is in the last resort a new expression of the ancient mystic principle of the identity of God and the soul and conceives all religion as self-realization.

In the Buddhist world we find also syncretistic movements. One of them is the Cao Dai movement which arose in 1926 in Vietnam among a group of civil servants who experimented with spiritualism.[91] The movement has a Pope, cardinal and bishops. It speaks of itself as a renovated Buddhism, but declares at the same time that it seeks to bring all religions back to their original unity. Among the principal guides whose messages are received by the leaders of the movement are Jeanne d'Arc, Descartes and Victor Hugo, which shows indeed a readiness to embrace all points of view. The movement had its own army and has played a considerable role in politics. It has a certain number of adepts in France and is in contact with one of the Japanese new religions, the Oomoto.

[89] Quoted in B. van Gelder, *Spoorzoeken*, Amsterdam, 1957, p. 109.
[90] *The Divine Symphony or Vandan*, 1926, p. 79.
[91] Maurice Colinon, *Faux Prophetes et Sectes d'aujourd'hui*, Paris, 1953, p. 84.

44

Besides this Oomoto sect, Japan has several other syncretistic movements. One of the most interesting is Ittoen, the Garden of Light. Its symbol is a swastika with a cross at the centre and a sun in the background. 'By the rays of the sun Buddhism and Christianity melt into one and form the circle of harmony.'[92] Its prayer is : 'Teach us to worship the essence of all religions, and help us to learn the one ultimate truth.' The leader Teno-san says that the faithful 'believes not only in God, not only in Buddha, or in Confucius alone, for he believes that all of their essence is within the gate of the one and only light'.

The African continent has also its syncretistic movements. In his well-known study, *Bantu Prophets in South Africa*,[93] Bishop Sundkler calls attention to the nativistic-syncretistic interpretation of Christianity in the African Zionist movement. Among the many independent churches and sects which have grown up in Africa there are those which simply seek to give a more specifically Christian expression to the Christian faith without departing from that faith. But there are others which have gone so far in re-introducing traditional African religious ideas and practices (sometimes including magic) that they have become essentially syncretistic.

Syncretistic bodies have also grown up in the Christian world. Besides a number of them that have not crossed the frontiers of their nation of origin we have especially three international bodies. The first is the Liberal Catholic Church. It was founded by prominent leaders of the theosophical society. One of them, C. W. Leadbeater, a man who was considered by the theosophists as 'one of the greatest occultists of our time',[94] wrote among others a book supposed to be based on clairvoyance and describing the 24

[92] Harry Thomsen in *Japanese Religions*, Vol. I, No. 3, 1959.
[93] Bengt Sundkler, *Bantu Prophets in South Africa*, 1961, p. 297.
[94] Preface to C. W. Leadbeater, *Orion*.

lives of Orion beginning in the year 23,875 before Christ.
But his conduct left much to be desired. The bishops of
the Church have a form of apostolic succession through one
of the '*episcopi vagantes*', but this succession is not recognized by other churches. The originality of the church is
that it allows almost total freedom of doctrine, but has an
elaborate liturgy based on the Catholic mass. According
to its publications Christ is thought of as having come to
the world again and again, 'founding one religion after
another, at the time and according to the needs of the race.
Thus it is thought that he was the inspiration for each of
the great religions of the world. . . .' So Jesus is an incarnation, but then on this view all men are incarnations.
Theosophy has swallowed the basic Christian affirmations.

Far more serious and significant is the *Christengemeinschaft* or 'Christian Community' which is as it were a
Christian edition of Rudolf Steiner's Anthroposophy. This
theology has impressive features in that it seeks to arrive
at an interpretation of the total cosmic process. But there is
no doubt that it has two sources of revelation, the Christian
Gospel and the 'gnosis' of Rudolf Steiner[95] which is a vast
synthesis of older theosophical occultist speculations with
the philosophy of nature of Goethe and with concepts of
modern science. Thus while it does not officially teach reincarnation, its leaders preach the doctrine of reincarnation
and karma. In its Christology it seeks 'to bring together the
historic Jesus and the cosmic Christ'. But it does so by the
anthroposophical construction of the union of a child which
represented the reincarnation of a person who had in many
lives on earth been a teacher of wisdom (e.g. Zarathustra)
with another child which belonged to humanity as it had
existed in paradise. Thus the story of the great deeds of
God is transformed into a record of cosmic processes

[95] *Evangelium und Christengemeinschaft*, ed. W. Stählin, 1953, p.
57. Cf. K. Hutten, *Seher, Grübler, Enthusiasten*, 1953, p. 401.

46

through which, exactly as in the old gnostic systems, the spiritual core of man is progressively released from earthly bondage. Thus it is natural that Christianity is here understood as a continuation and fulfilment of the ancient mystery religions. The gospel is forced into a framework which is foreign to it.

We must also mention Spiritualism, which operates mainly in traditionally Christian countries. In so far as it has developed as a specific religious movement, it has also definitely syncretistic features. This is particularly true of the elaboration of spiritualism made by Allan Kardec (France) in the 1850's and 60's. In his system the teaching concerning communication with the dead is the cornerstone of a theology which uses both Christian and Hindu conceptions. Spiritualism is a third and definitive revelation in the series of revelations of which Moses brought the first and Jesus the second. Hinduism contributes the doctrine of karma (cause and effect) and reincarnation.

It is in this form that spiritualism has become an organized religion. Its greatest success has been in Brazil, called 'the major spiritualist country of the planet'. A recent estimate is that there are more than two million adherents of spiritualism in that counry.[96] Now it is remarkable that this form of syncretism has again been combined with other religious elements in what may be called a syncretism of syncretisms. For the 'Umbanda' in Brazil is a combination of spiritualism with African religious traditions. As the 'Catechism of Umbanda' puts it: 'The Umbanda is a religious syncretism of African origin, incorporating elements taken from Catholicism, from spiritualism, from Indian religions.'[97]

[96] Candido Procopio de Camargo, *Aspectos sociologicos del espiritismo en Sao Paulo*, 1961.
[97] Quoted in 'Devant les Sectes non-chrétiennes', XXXI *Semaine de Missiologie*, Louvain.

Other religious movements, while not originally syncretistic, go so far in their adaptation to the various religions
that they become virtually syncretistic. Thus 'Moral Re-
Armament', by preaching 'change' without specifying the
religious content of that change, contributes to the syncretistic confusion of our time. Buchman has said that 'Moral
Re-Armament is the good road of an ideology inspired by
God upon which all can unite, Catholic, Jew and Protestant, Hindu, Muslim, Buddhist and Confucianist—all find
they can change, where needed, and travel along this good
road together'.[98]

*   *   *

We must conclude this all too rapid survey of the various
stages of syncretism. We have met with very diverse movements and very different people. And still it is remarkable
that we found in nearly every case the same basic motifs.
The many syncretisms have to a large extent a common
structure. Thus we hear a hundred times and in all languages that there are many ways to God and that God is
too great, too unknowable to reveal himself in a single
revelation and once for all. Syncretism is thus essentially
a revolt against the uniqueness of revelation in history.
True universality, it claims, can only be gained if the pretension that God has actually made himself definitely
known in a particular person and event at a particular time
is given up. Now a God who speaks in an infinite variety of
ways but never decisively really throws man back upon himself, for it is then up to man to determine how and where
he can reach ultimate truth. Thus the syncretisms conceive
of religion as a system of insights and concepts rather than
as a dialogical relation between a personal God and his
creature. They all tend to some form of gnosis, sometimes
of a more rationalistic kind, sometimes more intuitive or

---

[98] In an address given in Los Angeles, June 1948, reproduced in
Remaking the World, new revised ed., 1953, p. 166.

esoteric. They seek to realize salvation rather than to receive it. In this way they are, often unwittingly, contradicting their own claim to universality. For they in fact exclude those religions for which the revelation of a personal God is the central category.

One thing is certain. The Christian Church has not taken the challenge of world-wide syncretism sufficiently seriously. There is a famous statement of Gibbon: 'The various *modi* of worship which prevailed in the Roman world were all considered by the people equally true, by the philosophers equally false, and by the magistrates equally useful.' That statement can to a considerable extent be applied to the modern world, though there are now more of the people who think as the philosophers did in Roman times and more of the philosophers who think as the people did then. The magistrates seem to have changed least of all. Has it not been reported that Mr Eisenhower has echoed the words of Gibbon by saying: 'Our government makes no sense unless it is founded in a deeply felt religious faith —and I don't care what it is'?[99] Now the Church has been very much preoccupied with the many who think that all religions are equally false. It should become concerned with those who think that all religions are equally true. And this all the more since there is reason to think that not a few of these can be found among the church members themselves.

To take syncretism seriously means three things: first to know it, second to give a clear, theologically sound and pastorally relevant refutation of its errors, third to show that its concern for a truly universal faith is the concern of the Christian Church itself.

Our task in the following lectures will be to make a contribution to the giving of such an answer to the syncretisms of our time.

[99] Quoted by Will Herberg, *Protestant-Catholic-Jew*, 1955, p. 97.

II

THE NEW TESTAMENT'S STRUGGLE WITH SYNCRETISM

WE MUST now seek to describe how the New Testament deals with the syncretistic challenge. The first century is not the time of the climax of general religious symbiosis and confusion; that came in the next two centuries. But syncretism was already going strong. It is significant that by the time of the Emperor Claudius, contemporary of St Paul, the Egyptian and Syrian cults had already received official recognition in Rome. In Greece and the Near East the developments had been even faster. The writings of Plutarch, who was born about the middle of the century, show, as Lietzmann has put it, that all the gods of Egypt, Persia and Babylonia 'began, as it were, to speak Greek and take up philosophy and so became acceptable in every sense'.[1] For our purpose it is also important to note that at that time the Jewish diaspora was already deeply affected by non-Jewish religious thought and that its integrity was threatened by attempts to draw Judaism into the whirlpool of the general mixing process.

The primitive Church had to confront this syncretism as soon as its missionaries left Jerusalem to preach the gospel in other regions. It is remarkable that the cities which became the first strategic centres for the expansion of Christianity, and in which St Paul and his colleagues spent so much of their time and energy, were cosmopolitan cities where many different religions met together and entered

[1] H. Lietzmann, *The Beginnings of the Church Universal*, p. 266.

into close relations with each other. Antioch, Ephesus, Corinth and Rome had all opened their doors for foreign cults and somehow combined these with older indigenous forms of worship.

Antioch had its mixture of Syrian and Greek religion. It was one of the main centres of the cult of Adonis[2] and had also a temple of Isis.[3] Even its more official cult of Artemis and Apollo seems to have had more resemblance to the service of Baal and Astarte than to the worship which Artemis and Apollo received in Greece itself.[4] The orgiastic and sensual Maiumas festivals represented an ancient Syrian cult. Ernest Renan has given an almost frightening description of the endless religious and moral confusion which reigned in this place with its magicians, miracle-workers and deceitful priests.[5]

It was in Antioch, and probably in the time when St Paul spent several periods of time in the city, that Menander, one of the earliest gnostics and a direct disciple of Simon Magus, 'deceived many by magic arts'[6] and taught that through his magic he could even overcome the angels, who had created the world.[7]

In Ephesus the original and indigenous cult was that of the Great Mother, the Near Eastern goddess of nature who represented the abundance and fertility of the life-force. When the Greeks came to Ephesus, this older cult received a certain Greek varnish, but it did not change its essential character.[8] According to the Book of Acts (19.35) the people

[2] According to Lucian.
[3] See Baedeker's *Palestine and Syria*, ed. of 1912, p. 392.
[4] J. J. I. Döllinger, *The Gentile and the Jew*, ET, 1862, Vol. I, p. 432.
[5] In *The Apostles* (History of the Origins of Christianity, ET, 1889–90, Book II), pp. 118ff.
[6] Justin, *First Apology* 26.
[7] Irenaeus, *Against Heresies* I.23.
[8] R. Tonneau, 'Ephèse au temps de St Paul', *Revue Biblique* 38, 1929, p. 322.

of Ephesus believed that the representation of the goddess in the Artemision had fallen from heaven. Does this refer to the statue of Artemis (as is implied in many translations) or to a sacred stone (as the RSV has it)? Whatever it was, it is most probable that we have to do with a tradition concerning a fetish-like object of worship similar to the stone which was brought to Rome in 205 BC and which was considered as the seat of the Great Mother Goddess. Artemis herself was portrayed with a large number of breasts in order to underline, as St Jerome put it, 'that she is the nurse of all animals and all living beings'.[9]

The other cults in Ephesus belonged largely to the same sphere. We find Hecate and especially Bacchus. When Antony entered Ephesus, he came, as Plutarch tells us, as Dionysus (i.e. Bacchus).[10]

In addition to these cults, Ephesus became very early an important centre of emperor-worship, and the temple of Rome and Augustus was put partly next to and partly within the precincts of the Artemision. It is well known that Ephesus was also a great centre of the magic arts, so that all over the Near East magic formulae were generally called *Ephesia grammata*.

Ephesus has also a specific place in the history of syncretism because it was the place where Apollonius of Tyana, the first-century philosopher and miracle-worker, met with great success and was even worshipped. If we may believe his biographer Philostratos who wrote in the third century, Apollonius had travelled to Egypt and even to India to acquaint himself with their religions. He taught that all the various gods were expressions of the one supreme solar deity. But he combined this philosophical form of syncretism with magic practices. It is a remarkable

[9] In the prologue to his *Commentary on Ephesians*, quoted by Tonneau, *op. cit.*, pp. 321ff.
[10] In his *Life of Antony* 24, quoted by Tonneau, *op. cit.*, p. 353.

fact that this typical representative of the great mixing of the religions, whom some defenders of the old religions considered a much greater religious figure than Jesus,[11] was not only a contemporary of St Paul and St John but carried on his form of evangelism in the same city of Ephesus, where St Paul certainly and St John probably proclaimed the Gospel.

The city of Corinth at the cross-roads between the Eastern and Western parts of the Empire was the most foreign and orientalized of the Greek cities. Its main cult was that of Aphrodite, but not the Aphrodite of the Platonic *eros*, rather the nature goddess in whose worship the sensual element dominated. Even to-day we can recognize in old Corinth the streets where the innumerable sacred courtesans lived, right in the centre of the luxurious city. There were also the temples of the Phenician Melkart and the Phrygian Great Mother.[12] And then there was the cult of Isis whose festival of the sea was celebrated annually. St Paul may well have seen the noisy procession with its carnival features, its dancing priests and its gods in the shape of animals. It was in Corinth that in the second century the Lucius of the Apuleius novel was initiated in the mysteries of Isis. As we try to imagine that chaotic and wild religious life of the morally decadent metropolis we find it easier to understand Paul's reflections on idolatry, in the first chapter of the Epistle to the Romans, written in that city.

The fourth city which we must mention is of course Rome. By the middle of the first century it was in the first stage of the great Oriental religious invasion. The attempt of Augustus to bring the people back to the ancestral re-

[11] Thus Hierocles in his treatise against the Christians, quoted by Eusebius in his *Book against Hierocles*, ch. 4.

[12] See E. Preuschen on Acts 18 in HNT 4.1, 1912, also K. Lake and H. J. Cadbury in *The Beginnings of Christianity* IV (Acts: translation and commentary), 1933, p. 221.

ligion had failed. All cults and mystery-religions wanted to be represented in the imperial city and Roman soldiers, civil servants and business-men brought to Rome whatever new religious discoveries they had made during their journeys. The story has been brilliantly told by Cumont.[13] He has shown why and how the gods of the Near East, of Egypt, of Persia and Syria penetrated into Roman civilization and transformed the religious climate.

Now the small Greek-speaking Christian congregation, composed largely of people of Jewish background, will in those early years not have had much direct contact with the many newly introduced religions. But the syncretistic climate became increasingly important for it as it developed into a strong missionary force.

Some early conflicts with syncretism

Let us now look at some of the descriptions which the New Testament itself gives of the first encounters between the Christian Church and the syncretistic movements of the time.

At the very beginning of Christian missionary activity we have the conflict with Simon in Samaria. Simon Magus is a mysterious figure, but by combining the information we get from the Book of Acts, from the church fathers, from the gnostic writings and from archeology we can recognize a good many features of his personality. The Book of Acts presents him mostly as a magician, a man who seeks to manipulate supernatural forces. This is illustrated by his understanding of what the Holy Spirit means. He considers it as an additional and perhaps more effective source of power to be used in his professional activities. In businesslike fashion he wants to acquire the recipe from the apostles, whom he considers as colleagues or competitors. He does not realize that the *exousia*, the power or

[13] In *The Oriental Religions in Roman Paganism*.

authority, which the Holy Spirit gives is something radically different from the *exousia* which he wants to buy. This kind of power cannot possibly be added to the 'mana' of the magician, and the price is not money, but conversion.

But Simon was no ordinary magician. According to the Book of Acts he is known among the people as that 'power of God which is called the Great Power' (Acts 8.10, NEB). This means, as we can deduce from inscriptions of that time, that he was considered to be an incarnation or avatar of the great God.[14] Justin (who came also from Samaria and wrote about AD 150) confirms this when he reports that Simon was acknowledged and worshipped as the 'First God'.[15] But Justin tells us something even more revealing, namely that Simon was accompanied by a woman, whose name was Helena and who was said to be his 'First Thought'. Now it is a remarkable fact that there is clear archeological evidence for the existence of a cult of Helena in the first century in Samaria.[16] This Helena was a goddess of the earth and the moon, in other words a relative of the Phenician Astarte. Thus in later inscriptions she is called the 'All-Mother'. Simon may therefore well have been a priest of that cult and, after declaring himself to be a god, have associated with him an incarnation of the goddess Helena. Syncretism works in mysterious ways and by processes of association which modern rationalists find it hard to follow. In any case it is clear that Simonism is a meeting point for various religious currents. All of this would also seem to indicate that there is a good deal of truth in the ancient tradition that Simon was the father of gnosticism.

How did the early Christian missionaries meet this situation? They came with the 'good news about the Kingdom

[14] See Grundmann in *TWNT* II, p. 306 (*dynamis*) and *TWNT* IV, p. 546 (*megas*).
[15] *First Apology* 26.
[16] L.-H. Vincent, 'Le Culte d'Hélène à Samarie', *Revue Biblique* 45, 1936, p. 221; G. Quispel, *Gnosis als Weltreligion*, Zurich, 1951.

of God and the name of Jesus Christ' (Acts 8.12). Over against the speculations concerning cosmic forces which manifest themselves in innumerable ways, but never decisively, they set the announcement that God had acted once for all and that his Kingdom was at hand. Over against the many names they proclaimed the one name 'by which men may receive salvation' (Acts 4.12). To Simon, who desired to exploit the new religion and to add it in the best syncretistic style to his arsenal of spiritual energies, Peter said simply that the Holy Spirit is a gift of God, a gift that is given to those who repent, a gift to be used only in God's way and for his service.

Thus the keynote of the first confrontation with syncretism is the incompatibility between the service of God and the exploitation of his gift. The Gospel refuses to be inserted into the anthropocentric structure of thought and life which underlies the mixing of the religions.

Another aspect of the conflict between Christianity and syncretism is illustrated by the dramatic events which took place during St Paul's visit to Ephesus. In the city of the great Artemis, with its many pilgrims, the specialists of the magic arts had a flourishing trade. The worship of Artemis was often combined with the use of the *Ephesia grammata*, the esoteric and incomprehensible formulae which were supposed to have miraculous power.[17] It is curious to note that according to the Acts of the Apostles even Jews participated in such practices. Once again the name of Jesus was taken as a welcome addition to the magical collection. But Paul rejected this impossible confusion and as a result of his preaching there was a widespread reaction against magic and many expensive books of magic were burnt. A business man who seems to have held the key-position in the market for articles of piety, Demetrius the

[17] Tonneau, 'Ephèse au temps de St Paul', *Revue Biblique* 38, 1929, p. 357.

silversmith, became nervous when he saw his colleagues, the magicians, getting in trouble. Would his trade be the next to suffer? So he started a campaign against 'this fellow Paul with his propaganda' (Acts 19.26, NEB). The slogan which he adopted, namely that Artemis was in danger, was bound to be effective in a city, the whole life of which was centred in the Artemision. There followed a general riot during which the excited mob demonstrated against Christians and Jews. Finally the town clerk succeeded in quieting them down by telling them that they need not worry about the permanence of the Artemis-cult. How can a goddess whose image has come down from heaven be in danger? In any case no blasphemy had been uttered against her.

The town clerk may have been technically right in that, as far as we know, Paul did not attack specific cults by name. But Demetrius was equally right. For it is clear that Paul actually preached everywhere that 'gods made by human hands are no gods at all' (Acts 19.26). This is what he said in Lystra and in Athens. And this was a serious matter. If Paul had only come with the name of a new god it would have been all right. Only recently the divine Emperor had found a place close to Artemis. But to deny the reality and power of all the gods was unforgivable. And that was the common sin of the Christians and the Jews. For that would indeed undermine the whole basic understanding on which society was based, namely that there should be harmony between all gods and all men. Demetrius had seen further ahead than the magistrates.[18] He had understood that the proclamation of a unique revelation would have revolutionary consequences. What was at stake was nothing less than the question whether men should go on 'having faith in faith', that is in any kind of faith, or whether they should turn, as Paul put it in Lystra, 'from these follies to the living God' (Acts 14.15 NEB).

[18] Ramsay, *The Church in the Roman Empire*, 6th ed., 1900, p. 132.

3   A third illustration of the encounter between the apostolic kerygma and the syncretistic world is provided by the Epistle to the Colossians. I believe that there are strong reasons to consider that letter as having been written by Paul himself, but the discussion of that question need not detain us. For our purpose the important thing is to note how the men of the New Testament dealt with the pastoral problem of approaching Christians who were tempted by religious confusion.

It is clear at first sight that Paul had to deal with a church that was in spiritual danger. The danger did not come from the purely pagan world, but from a movement which sought to combine Christianity with extra-Christian concepts and that in such a way that the Christians of Colosse were tempted to consider this contribution as an enrichment rather than an impoverishment.

It is not too easy to identify those foreign concepts, for we have no other evidence than the epistle gives itself. But the main points seem to be the following.[19] The basic trouble is that the Colossians think that the Gospel of Christ can only save them from their sins, but it has nothing to say about their relation to the cosmic forces. Now they feel the need of guarantees concerning their status in the universe in addition to assurance concerning their personal salvation. So they add to their individual gospel a cosmic gospel, but they take the materials for the second from a religious philosophy which is based on presuppositions that have nothing to do with those of the revelation in Christ.

What are these presuppositions? They have to do with the 'elements' or 'elemental spirits'. This word *stoicheion*

[19] Although at certain points the analysis given by Dibelius in his commentary on Colossians (HNT 12, 3rd ed., 1953, p. 38) seems to go further than the evidence warrants, it seems to me more convincing than the somewhat too conservative exegesis of Ernst Percy in *Die Probleme der Kolosser- und Epheserbriefe*, Lund, 1946.

can mean simply the elements of nature, such as water and fire. But in the religious life of the time it had acquired a higher significance, namely the spirits dominating the world. In astrology the stars could be called by this name. Any force on which human life would depend could be considered such an elemental spirit. It was therefore inevitable that the *stoicheia* were considered as being intermediate powers between God and man and that they were worshipped as angels. We do not know just how far the Colossians had gone, but we hear St Paul definitely referring to the worship of angels (2.18), to special festivals (2.16) and to a form of ascetic legalism which was related to this special worship. There is obviously a Jewish element in this syncretism, for we hear of circumcision and sabbath observation. And it may be that Dibelius is right and that we have also to do with a mystery-cult. Some few indications point in that direction, but the question must be left open.

There can however be no doubt that this is a real syncretism in which the Christian faith has become mixed up with both Judaistic practices and cosmological speculations of Persian or other Oriental origin.

What is Paul's approach to this situation? It is first of all a pastoral approach. He recognizes the reality of the Christian faith of the Colossians. Instead of immediately condemning the heretical tendencies in their midst, he begins by a series of tremendous affirmations about the real significance of Christ. Without as yet referring directly to their cosmological speculations he proclaims the cosmic and universal Christ. In him all things—through him all things—for him all things. He is the beginning as well as the end. In him dwells all the fullness of God.

Thus Paul accepts the challenge. Do the Colossians think that they need something else than Christ to meet their desire for safety in the universe? But there is nothing else that has any independent existence. For, as Paul says (in the fine translation of the NEB): 'The solid reality belongs to Christ' (2.17). The elemental spirits are part of the world which Christ has overcome. Christians do not belong to that world, but to Christ; they have passed 'beyond reach' (NEB) of the elemental spirits.

So what is this syncretism? It 'has an air of wisdom, with its forced piety, its self-mortification, and its severity to the body; but it is of no use at all in combating sensuality' (Col. 2.23, NEB). To add something to Christ is really to take something away from him. Since he is the completely sufficient revelation, any attempt to improve the Gospel by the introduction of other revelations is really a denial of the gift of God. Paul took his stand against this syncretism—not simply by condemning it, but by demonstrating its irrelevance for those who knew the dimensions of the Christian faith. We may conclude with Dibelius that 'as Paul confirmed the cosmic significance of the faith in Christ, he maintained the exclusiveness of Christianity and saved the Christian Church from becoming just one mystery religion among others and from being submerged and overcome by syncretism'.[20]

4 Our fourth illustration comes from the Book of Revelation. One of the letters to the seven churches is addressed to Pergamon. It speaks of that city as 'the home of Satan' and as 'the place where Satan has his throne'. What does this mean? There are various possible answers. Pergamon had its famous altar of Zeus, but it was also a great centre of the worship of Asklepios, so often called *Soter*-Saviour, and it worshipped Egyptian gods. Moreover it was a centre of the Sabazios cult which had entered in a strange alliance with the Jewish worship of Yahweh Sabaoth. And, last but not least, it was the first Asian city to build a temple for Augustus and Rome. The throne of Satan has thus been identified by some with the altar of Zeus, by others with

[20] *Op. cit.*, p. 39.

the cult of Asklepios or with the cult of the Emperor. Strong arguments can be advanced for each of these identifications. Thus the symbol of Asklepios was the serpent, and this could be taken to mean that he was closely akin to Satan. On the other hand the martyrdom of Antipas, mentioned in this passage, seems to point to a persecution in the name of the imperial cult. Now it would seem that these various arguments should be combined and that we must therefore conclude that 'the throne of Satan' refers to the total religious life of Pergamon as an extreme example of complete syncretism.[21] The cult of the emperor is really part of the syncretistic system and gives syncretism an official status. The citizens are not asked to give up their faiths and rites, but to add one more god to the pantheon, though in a prominent place. This wider interpretation of the throne of Satan is confirmed by the fact that the main danger for the church in Pergamon is the heresy of Balaam, that is the temptation to compromise with idols in general. This points to something more than the problem of emperor worship.

What is the message of the Revelation *vis-à-vis* this syncretism? It is the judgment by him who has the sharp two-edged sword, the sword which is the decisive Word of God. The church of Pergamon has held fast his cause and his name, which is above every name. It has not denied him when it became clear that they stood before the ultimate choice: faithfulness and martyrdom or denial and earthly life. Now everything depends on maintaining their integrity. There must not be the slightest compromise with syncretism. The Lord himself will make war upon all who seek to have their cake and eat it. But those who remain faithful will receive the manna, that is the bread of life,

---

[21] So Schmitz in *TWNT* III, p. 167 (*thronos*) and Schäferdiek in *TWNT* VII, p. 161 (*Satanas*); cf. *Das Neues Testament Deutsch* on Rev. 2.13.

the white stone and the new name, which confirms their new citizenship in the Kingdom of God.

The keynote of this letter is therefore: resistance to syncretism up to the point of martyrdom.

Is New Testament terminology syncretistic?

We have seen that when the primitive Church encounters syncretism conflict is inevitable. The world which centres in the kerygma concerning the Lord Jesus Christ and the other world which makes room for an infinity of lords are in fundamental opposition to each other. But if this is really true, what must we make of the fact that there are so many conceptual and terminological links between the two worlds? Can it be that the conflict is more apparent than real? Has not the original kerygma, as it was passed on to the areas of hellenistic culture, been clothed in forms which are essentially syncretistic, and has this not resulted in a subtle transformation of the very content of the message itself?

These questions must be faced. For there is indeed a great deal of overlapping between the language of the New Testament and the language used by the religions of the Hellenistic period. It must often have come as a shock to young theological students when they first discovered that some of the central New Testament words are not the monopoly of the New Testament. I remember the surprise and dismay of an American friend who saw for the first time in his life the official Marxist slogans in the streets of East Berlin. His first reaction was: 'But they have taken our words.' Similarly some of the church fathers could only explain the identity of important biblical concepts with those of the pagan religions as a diabolical imitation. But apart from its inherent improbability that explanation makes the devil a prophet. For the fact is that many of the terms concerned were used in the pagan world *before* they were used in the New Testament. The famous inscription of Priene concerning the new calendar which is to take the birthday of the divine emperor as its starting point, which considers his birth the beginning of the world (*arche pantōn*), which speaks of him as *Sōter* (the New Testament word for Saviour) and of his birthday as the first of his evangels (*euangelion*) is dated 9 BC.[22] When Plutarch writes about Mithra as Mediator (*mesites*) he is almost certainly quoting from an ancient and therefore pre-Christian source.[23] On the other hand, if we find in Titus 2.13 the expression : 'the epiphany of the glory (*doxa*) of our great God and Saviour Jesus Christ', we cannot fail to see the close connection which these words have with the already existing terminology of emperor worship. These few illustrations must suffice to make the point that the problem of the relation of New Testament terminology (and consequently New Testament thought) to its Hellenistic environment is not artificially created by all too clever scholars, but is presented by the New Testament documents themselves.

At this point it is important to distinguish between several questions, namely those concerning the use, the origin, the purpose and the content of the biblical expressions concerned. We have in the many volumes of Kittel's Theological Dictionary for the New Testament, with its penetrating studies concerning the history and content of biblical words, a precious instrument which can help us in answering these questions.

First as to the *use* the New Testament makes of words which have general currency in the Greek-speaking religious world. It is of course inevitable that a large number of such words are used. As every Bible translator knows, it is impossible to communicate the biblical message without using a number of concepts which have already a specific history

[22] Wendland, *Die Hellenistisch-Römische Kultur*, p. 409.
[23] Oepke in *TWNT* IV, p. 608.

in the religious life of the people for whom the Bible is translated. What other word could have been chosen to speak of God than the word *theos*? But that word had of course its associations, many of which would be quite misleading from the Christian point of view. Now it is interesting to note that certain key-words of contemporary religious life were definitely avoided. They were obviously so heavily burdened with the wrong content that they could not be redeemed. A well-known example is that *eros*, a quite central notion of Greek religious life, is not used. The word is so typical of anthropocentric religion that it is inadequate for the faith in which the initiative comes from God. For the same reason *enthusiasmos* finds no place in New Testament terminology.

Other important expressions of the syncretistic environment are only used in a negative sense. This is the case, for instance, with *mythos*. The concept of myth, with its many pagan and syncretistic associations, cannot be filled with the content of the great deeds of God in history.[24] The New Testament itself makes this quite explicit. In the first Epistle to Timothy (1.4) Paul says that the interminable myths issue in speculation rather than knowledge of the 'economy of God', that is the plan of God. That 'economy' with its character of 'happenedness' is fundamentally different from the timeless stories of the religions of nature and mystery. For the same reason the Second Epistle of Peter (1.16) contrasts 'cleverly devised myths' with 'the power and coming of our Lord Jesus Christ'.

Or take the word *daimōn*. It is well known that the Greeks thought of demons as powers of divine origin and could therefore distinguish between good and bad demons. But the New Testament uses the word always in a bad sense and conceives of the demons as forces which are inimical to God.

[24] Stählin in *TWNT* IV, p. 788.

We must now turn to the *origin* of New Testament concepts. This is important because there exist a considerable number of expressions which belong *both* to the religious terminology of the New Testament and to that of the Hellenistic world. In trying to understand their biblical meaning our first question must be: from where did the New Testament receive these words? There are various possibilities: from the Old Testament, from later Palestinian Judaism (in which we must now especially include the Dead Sea Scrolls), from Hellenistic Judaism, from the non-Jewish Hellenistic world. The most important question would seem to be: Does the word concerned belong to the terminology of the Greek translation of the Old Testament as well as to the terminology of the Greek world? For if it belongs to both there is every reason to believe that it has come to the New Testament *via* the Septuagint and that it must be understood in terms of its Old Testament meaning. Several key-words belong to this category. Examples are *Kyrios* (=Lord), *Logos* (=Word), *Sōter* (=Saviour) and *euangelion* (=Gospel). There was a time when New Testament scholarship interpreted these words almost wholly in the light of their use in Hellenism. To-day the pendulum has swung back and it is now widely accepted that they are fundamentally Old Testament concepts and that it is the Old Testament background which explains their true meaning. We do not need the hypothesis of Bousset that the Hellenistic church in Antioch first began to call Jesus *Kyrios*, following the use of giving that title to gods and rulers. We have good reason to believe that the Palestinian church itself spoke of the risen Christ as Lord (Acts 2.36), that St Paul received this from the primitive kerygma,[25] and that they used it because they believed firmly that the God whom they knew from the ancient Scriptures, the *Kyrios*,

[25] C. H. Dodd, *The Apostolic Preaching and its Developments*, 1936, p. 24.

had come himself to the world in Jesus Christ and that therefore the *Kyrios*-title belonged equally to Christ.

In the same way it is not really necessary to suppose that the use of *euangelion* is due to its prominence in the Emperor-cult, for it has its roots in the prophecies of Isaiah. *Sōter*-saviour is also in this category, for it has a strong Old Testament background. And the same is true with the word, the origin and meaning of which has been more widely debated than any other word, the word *Logos*. Without entering into the many aspects of that problem we can note here that it plays such a central role in the Old Testament that it is impossible to detach it from that background.

This is not to say that the use of these words has not been influenced by their acceptability to the non-Jewish world. But it is to say that when they were used, they were used in the sense which they had acquired in their Jewish environment.

At this point the discovery of the Dead Sea Scrolls is of decisive importance. Many concepts and expressions which had until recently been considered as non-Jewish are found in the documents of the Qumran sect which was a specific expression of rigorous Judaism. This sheds a completely new light on the background of the Gospel of St John. As Professor Michel has said on the basis of this discovery: 'The idea that the fourth Gospel must be interpreted in the light of Hellenism or Oriental Gnosis should be abandoned.'[26] Professor Albright comes to the same conclusion and says even that the debate on the original background of the Gospel of John appears to be definitely closed,[27] a prediction which in the light of the history of New Testament studies may well prove to be somewhat too optimistic.

[26] In *Albert Schweitzer, Sein Denken und Sein Weg*, p. 127.
[27] Quoted in Jean Daniélou, *The Dead Sea Scrolls and primitive Christianity*, ET, Baltimore, 1958, p. 108.

Does the New Testament also use Greek religious terminology which has no Old Testament or Jewish background?
It does in a few cases. An interesting example is the word
'metamorphosis' which has a Greek background and plays
a considerable role in the religious philosophy of the time.
We shall therefore have to ask later what content and
meaning this word has in the New Testament. For the
moment we note that such Greek terminology is used more
often in the later New Testament documents, which belong
to the period when the Church went out to confront the
wider world.

More important than the question of origin is the question *why* certain words are used. What is the *purpose*
which dominates in the selection of New Testament terminology? Why is it that the biblical authors use so many
terms which the people of their time (or New Testament
scholars of later times) could interpret in a syncretistic
sense? Could they not have protected their message against
this danger? It seems to me that the answer is that they
could have protected themselves more than they have done,
but that they had good reasons for not thinking in terms
of safety first. These men were first of all messengers and
missionaries. They were surely concerned with the purity
of the Gospel, but they were equally concerned to make it
known and understood by the whole world around them.
So they were willing to take a spiritual risk. With remarkable courage and imagination they sought to get under the
skin of the pagan world and in order to do so they were
not afraid to use a great deal of the terminology which
they found in that world. Their method was really a combination of uncompromising loyalty to the central truth of
the kerygma with far-reaching readiness to make such ad-
justments of its form and expression as might be necessary
to reach the unevangelized. They had such a conviction
about the inherent power of the Gospel that they could

afford to go very far in using concepts which had so far had another meaning for their hearers. It looks often as if they put new wine in old skins, but what they were really doing was to put leaven in a lump of dough, so that the whole lump finally became leavened. They were definitely engaged in an offensive battle and sought to steal the thunder of their adversaries. It is a remarkable fact that the Book of Revelation, which represents the culmination point in the attack upon syncretism, is at the same time the book which uses the most 'syncretistic' language. The most fervent expressions of Emperor worship are used to make clear that Christ has the supreme authority. The images of Persian-Babylonian astrology are used to proclaim that Christ rules over all cosmic powers. Or take the Second Epistle of Peter. It uses several expressions which are unusual in other parts of the New Testament and come obviously from a Hellenistic background. To 'become partakers of the divine nature' is certainly a concept of Greek origin (II Peter 1.4). But this same epistle takes the most definite stand possible against a transformation of the history of Jesus Christ into a Christ-myth.

There can be little doubt that some key-words which are of Old Testament origin, such as *Kyrios* and *Sōter* (Saviour), are used so frequently and emphatically, because they could play an important role in the conflict with other religions. Both are used to some extent in the earlier documents, but both become far more prominent in the literature of the time when the young Church confronted the wider world with its many lords and saviours.

We must now turn to an even more important question, namely that of the *content* of expressions which the biblical terminology has in common with the syncretistic terminology. We take as our first example the word *mysterion* (mystery).

This is a specially interesting concept because it was used

both in the Hellenistic world and in the Jewish world, but not in the same sense. In the Hellenistic world *mysterion* means a form of cult in which the destiny of a deity is represented by sacred rites and in which the participants receive a secret initiation in order to become identified with the deity and with the cosmic forces represented by the deity.[28] In these respects the mysteries of Demeter and Kore (Eleusis), of Dionysus, of Cybele and Attis, of Adonis and of Isis have all one and the same pattern.

The Jewish world is not unaware of this Greek conception of mystery. The Book of Wisdom (14.23) contains sharp polemical statements against the mystery-religions. But the word is mainly used in the sense of a special revelation made by God himself about his plan for and action in the future. Thus Daniel says to Nebuchadnezzar: 'He who reveals mysteries made known to you what is to be' (Dan. 2.29; see also 2.28 and 47). It is also in this sense that the concept is used in the apocalyptic literature. The mystery is that which God has determined to do in the future. It concerns the final destiny of the world and of humanity. And in the Dead Sea Scrolls we find this same thought. In the Habakkuk Commentary the Teacher of Righteousness is described as the one to whom God has made known all the mysteries of his servants the prophets (VII, 4-5).

It is clear that there is a profound difference between these two conceptions of mystery. In the Hellenistic religious world mystery is a process in which through a certain form of initiation and cultic observance man receives salvation; in the Jewish world it represents an insight about God's design for man and the world which God bestows as a gift of grace.

Now in which sense does St Paul use the word? It is of course theoretically possible that he used it in the Greek sense. For he had certainly heard a good deal about the

[28] Bornkamm in *TWNT* IV, pp. 810ff.

mystery-religions as he travelled across the Mediterranean world. Certain scholars have therefore tried to interpret Paul's thought wholly or largely in terms of the mystery-religions.

But is this a justifiable interpretation? That question can only be answered by an analysis of the context in which he uses the word. And such an analysis leads to the definite conclusion that Paul's use of the word is based upon the Jewish tradition and not at all on the Greek tradition.[29] Whenever he uses the word he gives it a specific content which distinguishes it as sharply as possible from the syncretistic conceptions of the mystery-cults. What Paul calls a mystery is not a secret to be kept, but a divine decision to be revealed (Rom. 16.25). And the content of that revelation is not the timeless myth concerning a dying and rising god who represents the inherent vitality of nature, but the proclamation of the entering of the eternal transcendent God into history and the implications of that event for the destiny of mankind. In other words, in all places where Paul makes explicit what the mystery is, it has to do with God's actions which are part of the history of salvation. In the majority of cases the mystery refers to the whole mission of Christ (Rom. 16.25; I Cor. 2.7; Col. 1.26-27; Col. 2.2; Eph. 1.9; I Tim. 3.16). In other cases it refers to specific aspects of God's design such as the final conversion of Israel (Rom. 11.25), the calling of the Gentiles (Eph. 3.6), the coming of Antichrist (II Thess. 2.7).

The distance which separates the New Testament conception of mystery from that of the syncretistic movements becomes very clear if one puts side by side the hymn of the Naassene gnostics and the verses from ancient Christian hymnody in I Tim. 3. In the Naassene hymn Jesus says: 'Therefore send me, Father. I will descend, bearing the seals.

[29] Bornkamm, *op. cit.*, pp. 826 and 831. It is remarkable that St Paul does not use 'mystery' in connection with the sacraments.

I will pass through the aeons; I will reveal all mysteries; I will show the form of gods; and I will deliver, under the name of *gnosis*, the secrets of the holy way.'[30] Here Jesus is the revealer of secret knowledge which delivers souls imprisoned by the material world. But in I Tim. 3 the mystery is the incarnation. Jesus' coming in the flesh is the crucial event and men are not in the first place invited to know, but to believe.

This leads us to our next example. The word *gnosis* (knowledge) has of course its important Old Testament background. But it has at the same time a central place in Hellenistic and Oriental religion. Now a number of scholars have sought to interpret the Pauline and, more especially, the Johannine use of *gnosis* in the light of the incipient gnostic movements of the period. Do we really find here a door through which syncretism has streamed into the thought-world of the New Testament? There is really no good reason to think so. In fact there are strong reasons for believing that we have once again a case of the use of concepts which were current in the total religious environment (including the Qumran community), but which the New Testament uses in a sense which is specifically Christian.

This can be shown most clearly by comparing what the New Testament has to say about the relation between *pistis* (faith) and *gnosis* with the relation between these concepts in the other contemporary movements of religious thought. It is typical of gnosticism that *gnosis* is conceived as the highest degree of religious life. The truly spiritual man is a *gnostikos*, a possessor of secret knowledge. It is characteristic of the 'psychic' men that they live by 'mere faith and do not have the perfect knowledge'.[31] Now Paul

[30] *Gnosticism: an anthology*, ed. R. M. Grant, p. 115.
[31] Ptolemaeus, according to Irenaeus, *Against Heresies* I, 6.2 (quoted in *Gnosticism*, p. 175).

and John never contrast knowledge and faith in this manner. Paul, who had already to oppose a certain type of gnosticism in the church of Corinth,[32] does not hesitate to use the gnostic terminology. He also distinguishes between spiritual and psychic men and between those who have *gnosis* and those who have not (I Cor. 8.7). But this *gnosis* does not have the last word. *Gnosis* 'will vanish away' for it is 'partial' (I Cor. 13.8f.). But faith, hope and love will remain (I Cor. 13.13). And ultimately our knowledge will not really be our knowledge, but the reflection of God's knowledge of us.

Similarly John explains the meaning of *gnosis* by equating it with faith. When John 17 says, in v. 23, 'that the world may *know* that thou didst send me', this is a clear parallel to the words used in v. 21: 'that the world may *believe* that thou didst send me'. In several passages faith or belief and knowledge are combined (John 6.69; I John 4.6). '*Gnosis* is a structural element of faith.'[33]

And both Paul and John subordinate *gnosis* to *agape*.[34] *Gnosis* in the sense of speculative knowledge without personal commitment is not what God gives us or demands from us. True *gnosis* grows out of love (Phil. 1.9). Everyone who loves knows God, but the unloving know nothing of God (I John 4.8).

With regard to more specifically Greek expressions, like *metamorphosis*, the situation is not basically different. They are taken out of their Hellenistic structure and firmly set in the new Christocentric framework. They receive the Christian baptism and become vehicles of the theology of salvation centred in the divine events which have happened once for all. When Paul speaks of 'transformation' he does

---

[32] Bultmann, *TWNT* I, p. 709; ET, *Gnosis* (Bible Key Words 5), 1952, p. 42.
[33] Bultmann, *op. cit.*, p. 713; cf. ET, pp. 49f.
[34] Gaugler in *Jesus Christ im Zeugnis der Heiligen Schrift und der Kirche*, ed. K. L. Schmidt, 1936, p. 60.

not think of a mystical identification with a timeless process in the realm of nature;[35] he thinks in terms of that renewal which comes from entrance into the new age which has begun in Christ (Rom. 12.2).

We may therefore conclude that while there is a considerable overlapping in terminology between the New Testament and the syncretistic world, the substance of the biblical message has remained undistorted. Lietzmann says about Paul: 'It is of vital importance for understanding Paul's thought to notice that, no matter what forms of expression he used, they were never allowed to dominate their content; that content remained intact, and fully operative.'[36] But that is really true of the whole New Testament. There is remarkable audacity and imagination with regard to form, there is equally remarkable loyalty and consistency with regard to content. Cullmann puts the matter very clearly: 'Syncretistic elements, even myths, were indeed appropriated, but they were subordinated to a Christological structure which received its character not from syncretism, not from Hellenism, not from mythology, but from the *Heilsgeschichte*. It is characteristic of this structure that from the very beginning it centres in a real history.'[37]

The New Testament authors know that they can afford to go far along the road of communication, if one absolutely essential condition is fulfilled. That is, to use the words of Sir Edwyn Hoskyns and Noel Davey, that the Church remains subject to the historical control, the control by the Life and Death of Jesus.[38] New Testament 'orthodoxy' does not consist in an anxious holding on to specific forms of expression. On the contrary, the Gospel can and must be expressed in many different ways so as to be brought home

---

[35] Behm in *TWNT* IV, p. 766.
[36] *The Beginnings of Christianity*, p. 127.
[37] *The Christology of the New Testament*, ET, 1959, p. 322.
[38] *The Riddle of the New Testament*, 1931, p. 232.

to men of differing religions and cultural background. But New Testament 'orthodoxy' does consist in uncomprising holding fast of the central and unique evangel that God is in Christ and that the deeds of God in Christ are the crucial turning point in the destiny of man. As C. H. Dodd says: 'The great thinkers of the New Testament period, while they worked out bold, even daring ways of restating the Gospel, were so possessed by its fundamental convictions that their restatements are true to its first intention. Under all variations of form, they continued to affirm that in the events out of which the Christian Church arose there was a conclusive act of God. . . .'[39]

The answer to syncretism in confession and mission

The early Church expressed its faith in short liturgical or credal formulas, some of which we can recognize in the New Testament writings. In many cases these formulas are worked out for the purpose of use within the Church and have therefore no polemical intention. But sometimes they reveal how the Church responded to the challenge of the outside world. A significant example is the passage of I Cor. 8 where Paul probably cites an older confessional statement which he had received. Here the emphatic confession that there is one God and one Lord Jesus Christ is a specific denial of the divinity of the so-called gods and the true lordship of many lords. So here we have in one simple formula, which could easily be remembered, the answer of the ancient Church to all syncretism. How seriously the Church took this can be seen from the fact that we hear the echo of these words in Irenaeus' passage on the faith of the Church[40] and especially in the Nicene-Constantinopolitan Creed of the Eastern Church.[41] In that creed the

[39] *The Apostolic Preaching and its Developments*, p. 185.
[40] *Adversus Haereses* I, 10.1.
[41] See H. Lietzmann, *The Founding of the Church Universal*, p. 109.

Church confesses its faith in *one* Lord Jesus Christ in the same way as its faith in *one* God. The Apostles' Creed did not use the Pauline, but the Johannine formula, which is equally anti-syncretistic: 'his only Son our Lord'. The Greek is *monogenes*, and so points back to the classic text: 'God loved the world so much that he gave his only Son' (John 3.16).

It is, however, in the missionary consciousness of the primitive Church that we see most clearly how completely the faithful were convinced that they had received the one and only revelation, the proclamation of which was a matter of life or death for humanity. They did not merely want to propagate a religious conviction, they did not merely want to share a spiritual experience. They had heard the evangel, the news that in Christ the Kingdom of God had come, that God had offered his peace to man and that a completely new era, the last era, had begun. They were called to carry this word to all men. This is the *raison d'être* of the life of the Church and of its members. 'For if I preach the gospel, that gives me no ground for boasting. For necessity is laid upon me' (I Cor. 9.16). NEB makes the point especially clear: 'I can claim no credit for it; I cannot help myself.'

The two key-words used for the mission of the Church underline that the Church is not an institution which brings a religious message or makes an additional contribution to the spiritual life of man. The chief messengers are 'apostles', men sent out with a mandate by the Lord whom they serve. 'For how can men preach unless they are sent?' or 'How could anyone spread the news without a commission to do so?' (NEB, Rom. 10.15). The other word is to 'evangelize', that is, to fulfil the prophecy: 'How beautiful are the feet of those who preach the evangel, the good news' (Isa. 52.7). It was inevitable that many in the Graeco-Roman world understood this to mean that here was a *euangelion* that dared to put itself over against the *euangelion* of the one divine Emperor who incarnated the one empire blessed by the gods. Thus the missionary passion, not only of St Paul, but of the whole early Church, is in fact a practical demonstration against syncretism. And that is also the reason why the Christians were often considered to be atheists. When Pliny asked the Emperor Trajan for instructions as to how to handle these difficult Christians, the Emperor replied that all that is required is that they should agree to offer 'prayer to our gods'.[42] What could be easier? Syncretism can afford to be generous. But the Christians accepted death rather than this easy way out.

Did syncretism prepare the way for Christianity?

It has often been suggested that the great syncretistic wave of the first centuries of our era has paved the way for Christianity. Cumont says that the teachings of the Asian priests have against their will prepared the triumph of the Church. He illustrates this with the new interest in life after death, the new importance of the individual and the desire for a higher piety than that of the traditional religions.[43] Harnack speaks of the syncretistic processes as internal conditions which had to be fulfilled to make the universal expansion of Christianity possible. According to him the last phase of syncretism, namely the solar henotheism, was a secret ally of Christianity.[44]

But is this the truth and the whole truth? There is another and even more important side to this picture. It is that with regard to the central affirmation of the Christian faith, the affirmation that the word had become flesh, syncretism by its very nature was the strongest opponent of the early Church. A. D. Nock, who enumerates a number of aspects

[42] A. D. Nock, *Conversion*, p. 207.
[43] *The Oriental Religions in Roman Paganism*, pp. xxii-xxiii.
[44] *The Expansion of Christianity* I, p. 39.

of Christianity which in the time of expansion of the Church were accessible without too much difficulty to the wider public, points out that 'there was a substantial objection to any idea of incarnation—of God or a power of him taking human flesh and passing through birth and death, both seeming undignified'.[45] He quotes the *Corpus Hermeticum*: 'None of the heavenly gods will leave the bounds of heaven and come down on earth.'[46] In any case St Paul or the other early missionaries certainly did not think that the belief in many lords made it easier to believe in the one Lord. They had too much experience of Greeks who had turned down this new faith as foolishness. Many years later St Augustine, who had lived in the syncretistic atmosphere of Manicheism, had to confess that in the period before his conversion he considered Jesus as a man of high wisdom and could not understand what was meant by the incarnation.[47] To say that syncretism has prepared the ancient world for the acceptance of Christianity is therefore less than a half-truth. While it opened doors for the understanding of certain aspects of Christianity it kept the door closed for the acknowledgment of its basic affirmation. That is why the really systematic syncretists such as the philosopher Porphyry and the Emperor Julian opposed the progress of Christianity with all their might.

Is the New Testament a product of syncretism?

In the light of our preceding reflections it would seem unnecessary to spend more time on the question whether the New Testament itself must be considered as a product of syncretism. We have found that there is a deep gulf between the world of the New Testament and the world of syncretism. What then must we make of the fact that famous New Testament scholars from Gunkel to Bultmann assert that primitive Christianity is syncretistic? Gunkel

[45] *Conversion*, p. 236.   [46] *Ibid.*, p. 237.   [47] *Confessions* VII, 19.25.

affirmed in 1903 that 'the primitive Christianity of Paul and John is a syncretistic religion'.[48] Adolf von Harnack, who criticizes the '*religionsgeschichtliche*' school of Gunkel and Bousset for complicating the interpretation of New Testament concepts unnecessarily,[49] says nevertheless that as soon as Christianity entered into the pagan world it became syncretistic.[50] According to him the Gospel of St John is 'the most sublime representation of a certain syncretism'.[51] He considers that the combination of the Gospel with syncretism became perfected in the third century, but that if anyone had challenged the Church of that time to justify why it had allowed such innovations, it could have answered that it had but developed the germ which was planted in its being from the very first.[52]

We are concerned only with the question whether Harnack is right in qualifying the New Testament faith and message as syncretistic. Everything depends of course on the definition of the word. Now the difficulty is precisely that Harnack uses the expression in two different ways and for two phenomena which are essentially dissimilar. He has a whole chapter on the syncretism of the Hellenistic world and gives the following description of it: 'All existing materials were fused together, elements that lay far apart were solidified into a unity, and all previous constructions were shattered, while the surface of the movement was covered by broken fragments thrown out in a broad moraine, in which the débris of all earlier strata were found. This is the meaning of "syncretism".'[53] But when he speaks on the syncretism of primitive Christianity he defines it in the following way: 'From the very outset it

[48] *Zum religionsgeschichtlichen Verständnis des NT*, p. 88.
[49] *Dogmengeschichte*, 6th ed., 1922, p. 28.
[50] *The Expansion of Christianity* I, p. 394.
[51] *Dogmengeschichte*, p. 24.
[52] *The Expansion of Christianity* I, p. 396.
[53] *Ibid.*, pp. 32f.

78

(Christianity) had been syncretistic upon pagan soil; it made its appearance, not as a pure and simple gospel, but equipped with all that Judaism had already acquired during the course of its long history and entering forthwith upon nearly everything that Judaism lacked.'[54]

Is it not clear that these two passages use the word syncretism in very different ways? In the first we have the image of a blind force which obliterates all distinctions and leads to a total mixture of heterogeneous elements. In the second we have to do with the conscious appropriation and transformation of religious concepts from other sources. And it is of course significant that for Harnack syncretism includes the use of the Jewish heritage. As if there ever had been a time when there existed a 'pure and simple gospel' which was not rooted in that heritage!

It seems to me a most irresponsible use of terminology to apply the same qualification to the relativistic mixture of religions in which all revelations have more or less equal validity and are therefore interchangeable, as one uses for the New Testament faith which, while appropriating concepts and terminology from other quarters, remains firmly anchored to the one conclusive revelation in history. The similarities between the two are superficial; they have to do with expression and form. The dissimilarity is profound and has to do with the axis and the very substance of the two faiths.

Harnack himself has called attention to the term which was first a term of abuse against the Christians, but was later taken over by them as a true description of their mission: 'the third race'—'*tertium genus*'. They are a peculiar race because they do not accept the rules of the general syncretistic game. To obscure that fact by speaking of two syncretisms which are not essentially different is to misunderstand the gravity of the conflict between the early

[54] *Ibid.*, p. 394.

Church and its environment. To say as Harnack does: 'All it [Christianity] had to do with syncretism was to cleanse and simplify it'[55] is to miss the point of the struggle between the New Testament faith and syncretism, a struggle which has continued all through history.

The incompatibility between the message proclaimed in the New Testament and the thought-world of syncretism becomes particularly clear in the great struggle concerning the canon. The young Church is confronted with the issue what writings are to be recognized as truly apostolic, that is, representative of the original proclamation of the Gospel. But this is not merely a question concerning the historical origin of the many documents pretending to contain the teaching of Jesus and his apostles. The debate about the canon is not a debate between specialists in higher criticism. It is a debate in which, sometimes consciously and sometimes unconsciously, the question of the actual content of each document is weighed and weighed according to its degree of faithfulness to the original and central Gospel. Now in that debate the issue of syncretism plays a dominant role. The choice of the books which are to be included in the canon is a choice for the fully christocentric apostolic preaching and against all attempts to combine that preaching with elements drawn from other religious sources.

The great danger for the Christian Church in the early centuries of its life was not that completely relativistic syncretism which proclaimed the equality of all religions and created a pantheon in which all gods were welcomed. It was rather that more refined syncretism which is represented by gnosticism in its various forms. For the fundamental difference between gnosticism and the New Testament message consists precisely in the fact that gnosticism operates with concepts and ideas which have their origin outside the biblical world. Hans Lietzmann puts it clearly:

[55] *The Expansion of Christianity* I, p. 39.

'Among the gnostics the god of oriental mysticism rose up in power and might to contend with the Father in Heaven to Whom Jesus taught his disciples to pray.'[56]

There are many examples of overt syncretism in the gnostic literature. The gnosis which considers the Simon Magus of the Acts of the Apostles as its founder is really an attempt to fit biblical material into a Greek mythological framework.[57] According to Irenaeus the Simonians have an image in the likeness of Zeus and one of Helen in the likeness of Athena, and they worship these.[58] The Carpocratians have images of Christ alongside images of Pythagoras, Plato and Aristotle. They also believe in the transmigration of the soul.[59] In the book Baruch by the gnostic teacher Justin, Heracles and Aphrodite play an important role.[60] And the famous Naassene hymn with the exegesis attached to it interprets the coming of Christ in terms of the Phrygian cult of Attis and the mysteries of Eleusis.[61]

The gnostic literature which sought to compete with the 'orthodox' documents which were to become canonical is not so openly syncretistic. In the apocryphal Gospels and Acts the conceptions which come from foreign sources are more disguised. Thus the *Gospel of Truth*, the *Secret Book of John* and the *Acts of Thomas* transform the fatherhood of God into a combination of fatherhood and motherhood, but although there is no reference to any other religion, there can be little doubt that this 'infiltration of the mother principle'[62] is in fact due to the pervasive influence of the old fertility cults with their mother-goddess against which

[56] *The Beginnings of the Christian Church*, p. 295.
[57] H. Leisegang, *Die Gnosis*, 1924, p. 87 (French trans., 1951, pp. 62f.).
[58] *Gnosticism*, ed. Grant, p. 25.
[59] H. Leisegang, *op. cit.*, pp. 264f. (French tr., pp. 180f.).
[60] *Gnosticism*, p. 98.
[61] *Ibid.*, pp. 105-15.
[62] Samuel Laeuchli, *The Language of Faith*, Nashville, Tennessee, 1961, p. 33.

81

the Old Testament prophets had protested so strongly and with which St Paul had to contend in Ephesus. Again when in the *Gospel of Eve* Barbelo (the main emanation of God) says to man: 'I am Thou and Thou art I' we need no specific reference to oriental mysticism to understand that we have to do with the perennial monism typical of Hindu and much Near Eastern speculation rather than with a biblical conception.

In his recent book *The Language of Faith* Samuel Laeuchli has given a penetrating analysis of the deep difference which exists between the thought world of the Bible and that of gnosticism. The gnostic writers may use biblical vocabulary, but they use it in a different context. 'Peripheral speech permeates the center and becomes the center.'[63] In other words Hellenistic conceptions which are used in the New Testament as aids to communicate the Gospel of the great deeds of God in Christ now begin to play the dominating role. 'What makes Gnostic language Gnostic is the shift of center.'[64]

Gnosticism has lost the Old Testament perspective and the Old Testament is precisely the strong barricade against syncretism. Being concerned with speculative knowledge, it does not understand the central significance of the coming of Christ in the flesh and once for all. The conclusion must therefore be: 'To designate both biblical and gnostic language as "syncretistic" obscures the extent of two opposed atmospheres and misses the emphasis within the two.'[65] The choice of the canonical collection is fundamentally an act of spiritual discrimination in which the documents which proclaim the Gospel in terms which do not distort, but clarify that message are separated from the documents which give such prominence to foreign concepts that the Gospel becomes unrecognizable. The decision for the canon is a decision against syncretism.

[63] *Ibid.*, p. 39.   [64] *Ibid.*, p. 90.   [65] *Ibid.*, p. 90.

III

ONE FOR ALL
AND ONCE FOR ALL

WHETHER WE survey the history of religion or the present religious scene, we must come to the conclusion that there is more reason to say of the human soul that it is *'naturaliter syncretistica'* than to say that it is *'naturaliter christiana'*.

The argument for cultural understanding

The strength of syncretism has always been its inherent plausibility. This seemingly self-evident character has become immensely enhanced by the nature of our modern civilization. We live in a time in which the unlimited access to the cultural achievements of humanity has ceased to be the privilege of the few. In the realm of literature and art our minds travel to all epochs of history and all areas of the world. Thus modern man, whether he is a scholar or only a reader of paper-backs, has developed a catholic taste. He can love Mozart and Bach in spite of their difference. He makes a place in his life for Shakespeare as well as for Dostoievski. He receives inspiration from El Greco as well as from Rembrandt. More than that, he may well develop an interest in Etruscan, Japanese or Persian art. Or he may turn to the writings of Chinese or Indian philosophers. And all of these become part of his life and experience, all make their contribution to his conception of the world.

Why on earth should he not act in the same way with regard to religion and listen with equal curiosity and respect to the many varied voices of the mystics, prophets, religious teachers of all faiths? And why should he not build up a religious storehouse in which contributions from all sources are equally welcomed and all are used for the purpose of creating a comprehensive religious faith?

The case has been stated most persuasively by the Oxford scientist Dr Joseph Needham. In a sermon preached at Oxford and published in *Theology*[1] under the significant title 'Christianity and the Asian cultures' he makes a strong plea for the mutual understanding of the great civilizations based on 'the recognition that all mankind is one body and one spirit, under one God and Father supreme'. This involves for Christians the rethinking of their entire position in relation to the other great civilizations and religions of the world. What is needed is a new humility in the face of other religions. We must recognize the work of the Holy Spirit throughout the ages and in all cultures. 'The refusal to do this is the presumptuousness, the spiritual wickedness, which is one of the worst features of our Western culture.' In the presence of such spirituality as we find in the great religious teachings of Asia 'any preoccupation with the details of Christian orthodoxy in which we may happen to have been brought up is like turning the divine guest from the door'. The sermon closes with the quotation of a Sufi-hymn which says in part:

> 'O God, in every temple I find people that seek thee
> In every language I hear spoken, people praise thee . . .
> Sometimes I frequent the Christian cloister and sometimes the mosque
> But it is thou whom I search for from temple to temple.'

Dr Needham remarks that what he advocates has nothing to do 'with Comtism or Theosophy, or any other of those artificial mixtures or syncretistic brews of religious experi-

[1] *Theology*, May 1962, pp. 180ff.

ence'. This is true in as far as his position really implies that there is no need to mix different truths, since all with which he is concerned, Buddhist, Hindu, Taoist, Christian truths, are in his view reflections of one and the same ultimate reality. Why should one mix what is already identical?

The weakness of this position lies in the fact that it deals with religion as an element of culture. This comes out in the title and the several passages in which the words religion, culture and civilization are used as interchangeable terms. But none of the religions which are relevant for the world situation to-day considers itself as simply an expression of culture. Every one of them claims that it proclaims truth which transcends any culture and which is fundamentally independent from cultural developments, because it is not man-made but God-given truth. It is within man's power to change the content and shape of culture; it is not within man's power to change the truth that has come to him from God. To transform the struggle between the religions concerning the ultimate truth of God into an intercultural debate concerning values is to leave out the central issue at stake. In any case the Old and New Testaments do not merely deal with 'eternal values'. They speak of the decisive intervention of God for the salvation of man. And that can hardly be called a 'detail of Christian orthodoxy'. We can go along with Dr Needham when he asks for a repentant and humble attitude on the part of Western civilization, we agree with him in his plea for greater understanding among the cultures, but we cannot pay for these a price which amounts to the ignoring of the central affirmation of the faith, that God revealed himself once for all in Jesus Christ, for this would leave us in the confrontation of the religions with a gospel the heart of which would have been taken away.

There is this further point. When Dr Needham discusses

the problem of the relations between religions from the point of view of cultural relations he makes the same mistake which Dr Panikkar has made in his *Asia and Western Dominance*, that of identifying religion with the particular culture in which it has played the most dominant role. Now it is a fact that in doing so, these authors reflect a widespread attitude which has also played its role in the Christian Church and in Christian missions. But that interpretation which considered Christianity as an ingredient of Western civilization and missions as an instrument of Western cultural penetration was itself the product of a relativistic and superficial approach to the fundamental issues of truth. No living religion can ever be understood in terms of its cultural role only. To-day this misconception has also become an anachronism. Western culture is largely secularized. Even in the West the strongest cultural influences are out of tune with Christianity. On the other hand the Christian Church exists in all parts of the world. To think of Christianity as an expression of Western civilization is as much out of date as the colonial conceptions with which such thinking was associated.

The search for a common world faith

But does it not remain true that we need to-day more than ever a world faith which will provide an effective basis for human solidarity in a shrinking world? And is there any other way to arrive at such a common faith for humanity except through some form of syncretism? For unless we seek to harmonize the religions how shall we ever find that common 'ethos', that universally accepted system of spiritual values and moral principles which we need in order to overcome our babylonic spiritual and moral confusion, to end the war of ideologies and to give international law and morality a sound foundation?

We have already come across examples of empire-builders who produced new forces of syncretism in order to give their empires what we could call to-day a common ideology. Ptolemy of Egypt, the Roman Emperors Aurelian and Julian, Akbar of India were syncretists motivated by the conviction that a commonwealth, in order to have coherence and endurance, needs a common faith. The problem which these men faced has now to be faced on a world scale. As Max Huber used to point out, the fundamental weakness of the international situation lies in the absence of common norms to which all can appeal. International law cannot be truly effective as long as it does not have roots in common principles, and such principles depend for their life and vigour on convictions about the destiny of man. The declaration on the rights of man has a certain value even in the present situation, but can only become fully operative if it is interpreted in the light of a general agreement about the place of man in society and in the world.

This is a concern which cannot be lightly dismissed. It is of course true that there is a good deal of naive universalism. Some politicians seem to think that one can coalesce religions in the same way as business corporations. When the World Council of Churches was being formed, a prominent diplomat made the urgent suggestion that the Moslem world should be asked to join, for that would strengthen the front against atheism. There is however every reason to take seriously the warnings of the thinkers who conceive the problem not merely in terms of political opportunism, but in terms of the future of world civilization. Dr Radhakrishnan's concern to 'give the spiritual basis to a world brought together into intimate oneness by man's mechanical ingenuity'[2] must be shared by all who are concerned for the future of mankind. Dr W. E. Hocking is surely right in reminding us that to-day 'religion is and has to be cosmic

[2] *Eastern Religions and Western Thought*, p. 348.

87

business' and that a religion which is to give adequate guidance to 'the coming world civilization' must be a 'clarified messenger of the universal'.[3] Baha' U'llah, the founder of Bahaism, puts the same truth in poetic form: 'He who is your Lord, the All-Merciful cherisheth in his heart the desire of beholding the entire human race as one soul and one body.'[4]

The case for some form of universal faith is strong. But let us see what it would really mean. The present situation is that we have at least four major religions which think of themselves as religions with a mission for and to the whole of humanity. In addition to Christianity, Buddhism, Islam and Hinduism have developed a missionary consciousness and have met with a response which they consider encouraging. None of them (not even Hinduism with all its tolerance) would for a moment consider making way for another world religion. None of them is likely to become the faith of the whole of the human race within the foreseeable future. A world faith could therefore only be established if it were enforced by means of political or ideological power. But an imposed world faith would be a spiritual disaster and would be so weak in religious substance that it would not perform the function for the fulfilment of which it was created.

But can the great religions themselves not take the initiative to work out a common faith acceptable to the whole of humanity? They cannot, for that would be another form of suicide for them, and a suicide which they themselves would consider as a betrayal of their essence. It is true that some religions are remarkably hospitable to all religious ideas which will enrich their spiritual treasury, but even such religions insist that the imported religious goods must be used according to their own established norms.

[3] *The Coming World Civilisation*, pp. 84 and 86.
[4] *The Glad Tidings of Baha' U'llah*, p. 17.

In any case Christianity cannot possibly agree to become part of a world faith composed of elements of the various religions. This is not due to pride or egocentricity, but is simply the consequence of its nature and origin. It claims that God has revealed himself once for all and that man's calling is to respond to that revelation. Now if God has actually spoken and acted decisively that revelation cannot be compared to the objects of man's aesthetic admiration or scientific investigation. When God reveals himself man cannot say : 'I accept up to a certain point and on condition that I remain free to look around in other directions also.' He can only say 'Yes' or 'No'.

Syncretism does not know of revelation in that sense of the word. It may speak of many revelations, but this very multiplicity shows that none of them are in any sense decisive and that none of them demand a definitive commitment. So syncretism has no centre, no point of reference. Again it does not really harmonize religions, for it can only bring together the religions which do not believe in specific, concrete revelation. And when a certain religion of revelation does not fit into the harmonious scheme, the revelation which lies at its heart is treated as an accidental accretion and some of its peripheral features are declared to constitute its real contribution to the religious treasury.

This is clearly illustrated in Aldous Huxley's *Perennial Philosophy*. The author seeks 'the Highest Common Factor'[5] of all theologies, for this is the truly perennial philosophy, which is immemorial and universal. But the very first chapter bears the title, 'That art Thou', and thus we find once again that the stage is set for a forcing of all religions into the framework of the philosophy in which God and the soul are fundamentally identical. In this way it is of course impossible to include among the theologies whose 'highest common factor' is to be presented, any theology

[5] *The Perennial Philosophy*, 1946, p. 63.

which makes a clear distinction between the divine and
the human or any theology which takes its stand on the
unique revelation of God in history. The only form of Christian thought which is favourably considered is radical mysticism which, says the author, 'went some way towards
liberating Christianity from its unfortunate servitude to
historic fact', and which represents 'a spiritualized and
universalized Christianity'. He regrets, however, that in it
'the pure Perennial Philosophy has been overlaid, now more,
now less, by an idolatrous preoccupation with events and
things in time-events and things regarded not merely as
useful means, but as ends, intrinsically sacred and indeed
divine'.[6]

Thus its revolt against the uniqueness and concreteness
of a revelation in history leads syncretism to its own type
of exclusiveness and the perennial philosophy proves to be
just one religious position among others, rather than the
highest common factor of the relevant theologies which
have in fact dominated the religious life of the world. The
truth is, however unpleasant it may be, that in the realm
of religion all must choose between a number of positions,
several of which have from a purely historical standpoint
some reasons to claim that they are perennial.

The tragedy of syncretism is that, while it seeks to advance beyond the historical religions, it leads in fact to a
regression. This is very clear in those syncretisms which
seek only to harmonize the religions on the purely ethical
plane and present as the core of all religions and the one
thing needful a thin and watered down moralism. This is a
regression because it does not take account of the age-old
experience of mankind which shows that morals which are
not embedded in a structure of faith and ultimate meaning
are hopelessly ineffective. But it is even more tragic that
so much syncretism is really a return to the naturalistic

* *Op. cit.*, p. 63.

type of mysticism which was characteristic of the pre-Christian world. The less superficial types of syncretism tend to make man once more dependent on the impersonal cosmic forces. In the words of Nicolas Berdyaev they 'naturalize the divine mysteries'.[7] When Christ is no longer the one Saviour who liberates men from his enslavement to the forces inherent in nature and history, and when he becomes just one of the initiated among many, man remains caught within a closed universe. St Paul's battle had been to convince men that they were no longer dependent on the '*stoicheia*', the elemental spirits of the universe. Now these *stoicheia* seem to celebrate their return to power. The 'life-force' of D. H. Lawrence, the 'archetypes' of Jung, the 'spirits' of spiritualism, the '*karma*' of theosophy and other syncretisms are all impersonal powers which confront man with an 'it' instead of confronting him with the 'Thou' who is the living God revealed in Jesus Christ. There is no calling, no divine love (for love presupposes the I-Thou relationship), no hope. We are reminded of the words of St Paul to the Galatians: 'Formerly, when you did not acknowledge God, you were the slaves of beings which in their nature are no gods. But now that you do acknowledge God—or rather, that he has acknowledged you—how can you turn back to the mean and beggarly spirits of the elements? Why do you propose to enter their service all over again?' (Gal. 4.8-9, NEB). The post-Christian syncretisms with their pretension to go beyond Christianity are in fact pre-Christian and anachronistic, for they reject the liberation which the Gospel of Christ has offered to all men.

The demand for a world faith is comprehensible. But it must not be answered in such a way that we destroy the very foundations of faith. We must accept the fact that for a long time to come we will live in a world in which there will be different religions claiming that they have the

[7] Berdyaev, *Freedom and the Spirit*, ET, 1935, p. 274.

truth of God to offer. These religions will live less and less in watertight compartments so that more and more men will have to face the hard fact of the diversity of religions and make up their minds as to their own commitment. We cannot count on the emergence of one religion as the religion of and for all mankind in the period of history with which we are concerned. But this does not mean that we can do nothing about the concern that lies behind the demand for a single world faith. Much can be done to build common foundations for the world society that is emerging. We will come back to this point later in this chapter.

Syncretism's challenge to Christianity

In his discussion of theosophy and modern gnosticism, Berdyaev asserts bluntly: 'Christianity itself, or to put it more exactly Christendom, is responsible for their popularity.'[8] There is much truth in this, and it can be applied to many other forms of syncretism also. The Church has not done what it ought to have done to meet the challenge of syncretism. It has not answered the real questions which it asks. It has not taken seriously the very real concerns of which it is the advocate. It has not proclaimed the Christian faith as a universal faith, which will unite rather than divide humanity and provide a foundation for that common life which the nations and races must learn to live, if there is to be a future for mankind.

The Church has a pastoral responsibility for those many fine minds of our time whose comprehensive spiritual and intellectual curiosity leads them to make intimate acquaintance with many cultures and therefore with many religions, and who do not get any help in finding answers to their questions about the meaning of it all and about the relation of the Christian faith to this wide and rich religious universe. Take for instance the sensitive and brilliant

[8] *Op. cit.*, p. 288.

Simone Weil. In her *Lettre à un religieux*[9] she raises a formidable series of questions about the relations of the Gospel
to other religious teachings. There is no doubt that some of
these questions are based on syncretistic presuppositions.
When she belittles the Old Testament or denies the *raison
d'être* of missions, it becomes clear that she has not yet discovered the full implications of the Christian faith. But she
shows at the same time a remarkable insight into central
Christian truth. I think of her profound interpretation of the
cross as the intersection of time and eternity. So one cannot
remain unmoved by her challenge that, if her questions cannot be answered positively, she will have to be a Christian
outside the Church and that, in that case, the Church is
shown not to be truly catholic. It is high time for her questions, which are surely representative of the questions of
many of her generation, to be adequately answered.

The great tragedy of recent centuries has been that
Christianity has not really prepared itself for this new confrontation with the one world of our time. The relative
success of Christian missions in the last hundred and fifty
years must not blind our eyes to the fact that Christianity
has on the whole suffered from an eclipse of the truly universal elements in its message.

Berdyaev remarks that individualism is inherent not only
in Protestantism, but in the whole of Western Christianity.[10] It is perhaps better to say that in recent centuries
Western Christianity has been distorted by that individualism which came from the Renaissance. Many Christians can
only conceive of Christianity as a matter of individual edi-
fication and personal salvation and are completely blind to
the universal aspects of the biblical message. The churches
have not clearly proclaimed that the Christian faith has to
do with the ends of the earth and the ends of time, with

[9] Published in 1951; ET, *Letter to a Priest*, 1953.
[10] *Freedom and the Spirit*, p. 355.

93

mankind, with universal history, with the total 'cosmos'. The result has been that, just as the Christians of Colosse looked toward some extra-Christian mysteries for the cosmic insurance which they had not discovered in Christianity,[11] so modern men look to syncretistic movements for that wider dimension of faith which a purely individualistic piety does not offer them.

This situation is of course made more acute by the divided state of the churches. There is something almost ludicrous in the claim of Christianity that it has the answer to the demand for a truly universal faith, as long as it denies that universality by its internal divisions. There is undoubtedly a definite connection between the image which Christianity with its lack of unity and cohesion has given of itself and the growth of syncretism. If the Christian Church cannot really demonstrate that it is what it claims to be, the first-fruit of the new humanity transcending all human division and completely united by its Lord, then it is tempting to look in other directions for the solution of the problem of the spiritual solidarity of mankind.

There is a further complication. It is that so often Christians themselves give the impression that they consider Christianity as a species of the genus religion, as a subdivision of the general human preoccupation with the divine. Now it is inevitable that if Christianity is presented in that fashion, the conclusion is drawn that religion is universal and that Christianity is only one of its particular expressions. Since the eighteenth century, and especially since Schleiermacher, this reduction of Christianity to a province of the wide empire of religion has become so widely accepted that most Christians are shocked and surprised when they are told that this view of Christianity is a modern invention which has no foundation whatever in the Bible. Karl Barth has said, 'Neo-Protestantism is religion-

[11] Dibelius on Colossians (HNT 12), p. 39.

ism', for it has systematically sought to interpret the Christian faith in categories which were taken from a general philosophy of religion rather than in categories provided by the Christian faith itself.

Is then Christianity not a religion? It is one from the point of view of the observer who looks at it from the outside and who has a perfect right to compare it with other religions. It is not one from its own point of view. Christianity understands itself not as one of several religions, but as the adequate and definitive revelation of God in history. To classify this faith as one of the expressions of a general phenomenon called religion is to set it in a framework which is foreign to its nature.

One cannot exaggerate the confusion created by modern terminology in this respect. Every time Christians use the word religion meaning something wider than Christianity, but including Christianity, they contribute to the syncretistic mood of our times and strengthen the conviction that the truly universal force is religion, not Christianity.

Now the truth is that religion in the singular does not exist. John Haynes Holmes says: 'Religion has not many voices, but only one.'[12] But where is that one voice? In fact we hear voices which contradict each other at the most fundamental points. The book from which we take this quotation goes so far as to include 'Karl Marx and the Religion of Communism' among the world religions. But to declare that Christians and Marxists speak with one voice is to live in a world of make-believe.

It is high time that Christians should rediscover that the very heart of their faith is that Jesus Christ did not come to make a contribution to the religious storehouse of mankind, but that in him God reconciled the world unto himself. It is time for the Church to pay the unpaid bill which

[12] In the preface to *World Religions and the Hope for Peace* by David Rhys Williams, Boston, 1951.

syncretism represents. It is time to show that there is inherent in the Gospel a universalism *sui generis*.

What is Christian universalism?

Let us try to describe the nature of that specific universalism which is rooted in the Gospel.

It has its source and foundation in one person: Jesus Christ. The New Testament is not unmindful of the fact that this concentration of the whole history of salvation in one single individual does not fit into the accepted categories of Jews and Greeks, of religion and philosophy. But it considers this central truth so essential that it cannot be stated too often or too emphatically. In every part of the New Testament, in every stage of the early tradition, we find that the coming of Jesus Christ has completely transformed the human situation. Man's eternal destiny depends on his decision concerning the relation to this one Jesus of Nazareth. It is because of him that the whole outlook for the future has changed. It is through him that a totally new community is formed.

This person is completely unique. There is only one teacher, the Christ (Matt. 23.10), one Lord (Eph. 4.5; I Cor. 8.6), one shepherd (John 10.16), one mediator (I Tim. 2.5). He has a name which is above every name (Phil. 2.9). He is the only Son (John 3.16). Every one of the christological titles signifies that he has a mission that no one else has ever had or will ever have. 'There is no other name granted to men, by which we may receive salvation' (Acts 4.12, NEB).

He has come at a particular moment of history. He enters into the life of humanity. He is not an idea, not a principle, not a myth. He is tempted. He suffers on the Cross. He dies and is buried. His story is an event in the historical sequence of events. The coming of Jesus Christ has happened once upon a time.

But this 'once' has still another dimension. It is not merely a *moment* of history; it is also the *centre* of history. When the Word becomes flesh, when God 'in this the final age' speaks to men in the Son (Heb. 1.2), when Christ arises from the dead, this means that the crucial divine intervention has taken place. Christ has not only come once upon a time, but once for all (Rom. 6.10; Heb. 7.27 and 9.28; I Peter 3.18). There cannot be other incarnations.

How seriously this definitive character of the work of Christ is taken becomes especially clear in the fifth chapter of Romans. Here we find the synthesis of all the foregoing. There is the almost monotonous repetition that just as there has been one Adam, so there is one second Adam. We hear that this one man is unique in that he incarnates the grace of God; that he is a true man, a historical person. And it is made clear that his coming means a complete change in the situation of mankind, in that he brings new life and inaugurates the new and final era of history.

It is very important that the only person with whom Paul compares Jesus is Adam (see also I Cor. 15). Adam is the prototype who foreshadows Jesus Christ. Why? Because Adam is the father of the old humanity as Christ is the father of the new humanity. With Adam the first book of history is opened; with Christ the second and final book begins. We live under the shadow of Adam's life, we are called to live in the light of Christ's life. But here we see that the comparison breaks down. For 'the gift of God is not to be compared in its effect with that one man's sin' (Rom. 5.16). In a deeper sense Christ stands over against Adam, as grace stands over against condemnation, as obedience stands over against disobedience, as life stands over against death, as the new age stands over against the old age.

Is this merely speculation and, for that matter, a speculation based on ancient Oriental myths about a heavenly man who is at the same time the Saviour? Certainly not for Paul or for the primitive Church. If he has used concepts which had played a role in Oriental and Jewish speculation he has transformed them altogether. For instead of identifying the original man with the Saviour, he shows the fundamental contrast between Christ and Adam, and the man whom he proclaims as Saviour is not an idea, but the Jesus Christ of history who within the old history has opened the way for the new history.[13] This is not speculation, but interpretation of universal history from the point of view of the faith that Jesus Christ is the first-fruit of the new creation. And that faith is based on the original kerygma. Had not Jesus in identifying himself with the Son of Man and with the suffering Servant made this interpretation inevitable? Cullmann points out that 'the idea of representation is common to both the *barnasha* [Son of Man] and the *ebed Yahweh* [Servant of God]'[14] and that 'Paul united the two basic concepts Son of Man and Servant of God exactly as Jesus united them'.[15] There is a majestic simplicity about this view. Two great types who represent two opposing forces dominate all history. We are asked to choose between the life identified with the old man and the life identified with the new man, between living in Adam and living in Christ.

So far it would seem that the New Testament is almost exclusively concerned to concentrate everything on one centre, on one single person, one divine event, in a formidable reduction of the rich variety of human possibilities to an exceedingly narrow faith. But there is another side. It is, as Romans 5 makes so very clear, that this narrow door opens on the wide horizons of a true universalism. The chapter concerning the uniqueness of Christ is also the

[13] See Oepke in *TWNT* II, p. 538 (*en*), and Althaus in *Das Neues Testament Deutsch* II (commentary on Romans), 6th ed., 1953, p. 204.
[14] Cullmann, *Christology of the New Testament*, p. 161.
[15] *Ibid.*, p. 171.

chapter concerning the many, concerning all men (vv. 18 and 19). Paul's preoccupation with the one Saviour does not make him forget humanity. On the contrary the one leads inevitably to the many.

This togetherness of the one man with mankind is found in many New Testament passages. Romans 5 repeats three times that the one man has come to save the many (or all men). According to I Tim. (2.5) the one mediator wins freedom for all mankind. Heb. 9.28 speaks of Christ who has been offered once to bear the sin of many, and II Cor. 5.14 has the shortest and simplest formulation: 'one died for all'. What is the relation between the one and the many? It is all included in the little word 'for'. One has carried the burden of all, suffered for all, died for all. The second Isaiah had already proclaimed this. 'He bore the sin of many' (53.12). Jesus himself had described his mission as giving his life as a ransom for many (Mark 10.45; 14.24). And, though he confined his mission during his life to the people of Israel, the clear implication of his teaching concerning the Kingdom of Heaven (Matt. 8.11), concerning the universal role of the Servant of God (Matt. 12.18), and of the Son of Man (Matt. 25.31ff.) is that after his death salvation is to be proclaimed to all men.[16] John (12.32) gives the explicit statement: 'I, when I am lifted up from the earth, will draw all men unto myself.'

So Paul stands on a firm foundation when he concludes that this one man's life and death and resurrection cannot be understood in terms of an individual existence. It has its significance in its identification with and sacrifice for the many.

But who are these 'many'? The question is important. Must we say that Jesus died for a certain number of men or rather that he died for mankind as a whole? There can be no question that Paul means to say that the one died for

[16] See J. Blauw, *Gottes Werk in dieser Welt*, pp. 75ff.

99

all mankind. This is clearly stated in several of the places
we have mentioned and where Paul uses the word 'all'. But
even the places where the word 'many' is used must be
interpreted in this wide and universal sense. This is proved
by the fact that Paul puts in Rom. 5 the sentences which
speak of the offer of salvation to the many in a clear
parallelism with phrases concerning the offer of salvation
to all men. Joachim Jeremias has shown[17] that practically
everywhere in the New Testament in the passages concerning the death of Christ for the many the meaning is that he
died for all. Paul's proclamation that God was reconciling
the world to himself and John's statement that the lamb
carries the sins of the world are therefore representative of
New Testament theology as a whole.

Since Christ died for all, all have died (II Cor. 5.15). That
is to say: the old humanity is *passé*, antiquated. The time
of the new creation, the new humanity, has come. The
meaning of the age in which we live now is that the work
of reconciliation which was begun in Christ must still be
completed. There are those who have understood what
God has done and who accept gratefully the gift of
reconciliation. There are those who do not accept and
those who have not yet heard the good news. So the word
'all' is now used in two different connotations. Paul says:
'The same Lord is Lord of all', that is to say of the whole of
humanity, but he continues: 'and bestows his riches upon
all who call upon him' (Rom. 10.12), that is to say on those
who fulfil the one condition of responding to the good
news. As men take their decision for or against him a distinction arises between those who realize the crucial significance of God's deed in Christ and those who do not. There
is the realized universalism of the Church, representing the
new humanity, which precisely because it represents that
humanity, must be described in terms of wholeness as in

[17] In *TWNT* VI, pp. 541f. (*polloi*).

22851

I Cor. 12, where the underlying motif is that all (or the many) are one body. And there is the universalism yet to be realized which will find its fulfilment in 'the reconciliation of the world' (Rom. 11.15).

This means that the universal Church has as such a double function. First of all it must in its own life manifest the universality which characterizes the new reconciled humanity. It represents 'the one new man' (Eph. 2.15). In it the old dividing walls have been broken down. Christ is 'all and in all' (Col. 3.11) and the Christian family is 'all one in Christ Jesus' (Gal. 3.28). This oneness and universality is not merely a desirable quality of its life; it is an essential part of its mission. Eph. 4 is not a counsel of perfection; it is a description of the nature and mission of the Church. The unity of the spirit is to be maintained, because it is the necessary expression of that uniqueness, that unity and that universality which characterize the Church as the new humanity.

The second function of the universal Church is to be the messenger of God's universal offer of reconciliation. The 'all', who are one in Christ, exist for the sake of the 'all' for whom Christ died, but who do not know or acknowledge him. The appeal which God makes to humanity is made through ambassadors, through 'us' (II Cor. 5.20). They are to make 'disciples of all nations' (Matt. 28.9). Through them the prophecy is realized that 'their voice has gone out to all the earth and their words to the ends of the *oikoumene*' (Rom. 10.18, based on Ps. 18.5). The realized universalism stands in the service of the wider universalism of the history of salvation which continues. Christ is the centre of two concentric circles, the circle which represents the Church and the circle which represents humanity. The smaller circle must become wider and wider. The situation remains dynamic. The divine act on which reconciliation depends has happened once for all and is unrepeatable, but the ministry of reconciliation is to go on till the end of time. The Church is the missionary Church, because it is the instrument of God's world-embracing plan of salvation. In the Epistles to the Colossians and to the Ephesians the full implications of the Church's place in that plan become visible. Since the work of Christ has cosmic dimensions, the Church itself has a cosmic role to fulfil.[18] How shall it do this, unless it manifests universality, both in its own life and in its active missionary concern for the salvation of all mankind and for the reconciling of all things to God?

New Testament universalism is therefore characterized by the fact that in it the central figure, the body which he creates and the humanity for whom he has given his life, belong together and are inseparable. Uniqueness, unity and universality are all indispensable and mutually interdependent. There is no universality if there is no unique event. But the unique event is not realized in its significance, where there is no movement forward and outward toward universality. And the link between the two is in the body which in its unity, transcending all divisions, is the first fruit of the new humanity.

We have to do with a real universalism which, however, does not have its point of departure in a conception of man or of religion in general, but in the great deeds of God in history. We may call it a concrete universalism, because its character is the expansion of a concrete, historical reality.[19] This Christocentric universalism stands for the truth that humanity by itself cannot realize its desire for true universality. Only when it accepts the cross of Christ

[18] It is a remarkable fact that of the three longer passages in which the 'universalist' words *pantes, panta* or *polloi* play such a dominating role, one (I Cor. 12.12-26) deals with the meaning of universality for the life of the Church, one (Rom. 5.12-19) with its meaning for the life of mankind, and one (Col. 1.15-23) with its cosmic meaning.

[19] Oepke, *Das neue Gottesvolk*, pp. 121f.

as the centre of its life the way is opened for the overcoming of the forces that divide men from each other. 'If
we walk in the light, as he is in the light, we have fellowship one with another' (I John 1.7).

The New Testament presents, as Théo Preiss has put it,
'the vision of a veritable humanism which is at the same
time very exacting, narrow in its point of departure, the
(one) Man, but infinitely vast in its inclusive sense'.[20]

The rediscovery of Christocentric universalism in the ecumenical movement

The ecumenical movement of our time is an attempt to
realize this specific Christian universalism. The story of the
development of that movement shows how it discovered
progressively the different constituent elements of that universalism and their fundamental interdependence. That
discovery has taken a long time and is still going on. Strong
resistance has had to be overcome. A bird's eye view of the
history of the ecumenical movement from this perspective
will help us to see more clearly what has been achieved
and how much remains to be done.

The World Missionary Conference of 1910 had the wide
perspective of the total missionary task. Its chairman, John
R. Mott, will always be remembered as the man who not
only proclaimed, but embodied in his life, the universal
dimension of the gospel of Christ. Karl Barth wrote in 1911
about Mott: 'This is Mott's personality: something happens. And what happens is not just anything, but at once
the ultimate and most important thing that can happen:
man is judged by his aim and the aim is mankind.'[21] The
Edinburgh Conference reflected this preoccupation with the
world-wide evangelization of the whole world as the one
urgent Christian task. So the Edinburgh Conference gave a

[20] Théo Preiss, *Le Fils de l'Homme* (Suite), p. 65.
[21] Reprinted in *Ecumenical Review*, April 1955, p. 260.

clear witness to the world-embracing nature of the Christian faith. Nevertheless it did not give a complete witness concerning the nature of Christian universalism. For the resolution about the continuation of the Conference said specifically that this continuation was to follow the lines of the Conference itself 'which are interdenominational and do not involve the idea of organic and ecclesiastical union'. Because of the resistance in many missionary circles against any relationship that might lead to a unity in doctrine, this restriction was at the time inevitable. But by thus preventing all discussion on matters of faith and order the International Missionary Council (which grew out of the Edinburgh Conference) could not give a clear interpretation of the nature of Christian universalism which includes, as we have seen, the witness to the unity of the people of God. It is also remarkable that the Council did not adopt a specific basis, but simply said that 'it is recognized that the successful working of the International Missionary Council is entirely dependent on the gift from God of the spirit of fellowship, mutual understanding, and desire to co-operate'. In the official documents no explicit statement concerning the Christocentric character of Christian universalism was made. In the case of a missionary body this was less serious than it would have been elsewhere, because practically all missionary agencies took their stand on the foundation of a Christocentric faith. But it meant that the Council could not present a coherent conception of the nature of a specifically Christian universalism.

As the years went by, the themes which had been at first considered too dangerous, began to knock on the doors of the IMC. At the Tambaram meeting of 1938, with its strong emphasis on the Church, the issues of unity and the theological issues in general took a very prominent place. It was increasingly seen that the universalism of world evangelization needed to be based on the two other great components of Christian universalism: the common affirmation of the centrality of Christ and a common conception of the nature and task of the Church. Thus the Council was increasingly prepared to join with other parts of the ecumenical movement which had in their own way discovered the full implications of Christian universalism.

Almost immediately after the Edinburgh Conference of 1910 Bishop Brent, who had been deeply impressed by that conference, began to organize the 'Faith and Order' movement. He felt that there was need for a body which would specifically deal with the questions of visible unity. He shared the vision of Mott, but was convinced that Christianity would not and could not perform its universal mission as long as it remained so hopelessly divided. Now Faith and Order emphasized precisely those aspects of universalism which the missionary movement had not been able to emphasize. Brent and his associates realized that, as they sought to bring the churches together in conference to consider the question of visible unity, they had to answer the question what should be the nature and scope of that unity. They could not of course make an *a priori* choice between the differing conceptions of unity held by the various Christian traditions. But they could try to indicate what they believed to be the distinctive character of church unity as compared with secular concepts of unity. It is well known that they decided to address their invitation to churches 'which accept our Lord Jesus Christ as God and Saviour'.

This decision has often been interpreted as a device to exclude certain groups of churches. But its purpose was in the first place positive. It was a choice for Christocentric unity over against a vague and undefined unity, a choice for the unity given once for all in and by Jesus Christ as God incarnate. It was not a choice for an introverted orthodoxy. Bishop Brent, who was an active fighter for world peace, and took a great share in the struggle against the opium trade, had none of the characteristics of a narrow ecclesiastic.

The remarkable layman who translated the 'Faith and Order' plan of Bishop Brent into reality, Robert Gardiner, explained again and again the real significance of the Basis. It was functional, for it had to do with the nature of the unity that was envisaged. Thus Gardiner said at one of the early Faith and Order meetings in 1915 : 'The reason for the restriction of the Conference to those Communions throughout the world which confess our Lord Jesus Christ as God and Saviour must be made plain. Our attempt is not simply to promote kindly feeling or good fellowship, or even good works, but to reunite all Christians in the one living Body of the one Lord, both God and man, incarnate, crucified, buried, risen from the dead and ascended on high, living to-day, the Head over all things to the Church which is his Body, the fulness of him that filleth all in all.'[22] And in 1919 Gardiner wrote to Dr Siegmund Schultze : 'It seems to us that the conception of Christian unity held by those who accept that fact and doctrine (i.e. the Incarnation) must be totally different from that of those who regard our Lord only as a great religious teacher. Moreover, we believe that the only hope for the future of the world rests in that visible unity of Christians which shall manifest to the world God incarnate in the person of his Son, in Jesus Christ, manifesting himself in infinite love, that his new commandment that we should love one another even as he has loved us, may be the fundamental obligation of mankind in every relation, international, social and industrial.'[23]

These two statements show that when these early Faith and Order leaders spoke of Jesus Christ, God and Saviour, they meant the incarnation. It is not difficult to criticize

[22] *Faith and Order Pamphlet* No. 30, p. 17.
[23] The original of this letter is in the 'Oekumenische Archiv' in Soest (Germany).

their choice of words. But we can only be grateful for their insistence that the unity and universality with which the ecumenical movement must be concerned can only be the one that is created by Jesus Christ himself as the one in whom God reconciles the world to himself.

Just as the historic deed of the fathers of Edinburgh had been to give a clear, concrete witness to the objective of universalism—the proclamation of salvation in Christ to all men—so the fathers of Faith and Order gave a definite witness to its centre, the one Jesus Christ who is the author of both unity and universality.

Faith and Order continued to concentrate on this central truth. The affirmation of Unity of the Edinburgh Conference of 1937 says: 'This unity does not consist in the agreement of our minds or the consent of our wills. It is founded in Jesus Christ himself, who lived, died and rose again to bring us to the Father and who through the Holy Spirit dwells in his Church. We are one because we are all the objects of the love and grace of God, and called by him to witness in all the world to his glorious Gospel.'

But Faith and Order's witness was also incomplete. By concerning itself exclusively with the issues of church unity it was in danger of forgetting the objective of that unity. It raised the question of the unity that is in Christ without setting that question sufficiently in the context of the universal work of Christ in and for mankind. It also needed to be inserted in a wider framework. Faith and Order understood this increasingly and thus became prepared for an integration with other parts of the ecumenical movement.

The 'Life and Work' movement, which became widely known through the Stockholm Conference of 1925, was due to the initiative of Archbishop Söderblom of Sweden. He had felt deeply about the impotence of the Church to stem the tide of hatred during the First World War. His was a burning desire to unite the different churches in the application of the Spirit and teaching of Christ to social, national and international relationships. Thus 'Life and Work' became a movement for 'practical Christianity' and excluded from its deliberations the issues of faith and order. Here then we have another form of Christian universalism, an attempt to proclaim the lordship of Christ in all realms of life. Although such claims as that Stockholm represented the 'Nicaea of ethics' went a good deal too far, it was no small thing that representatives of so many churches spoke out together for the validity of Christian principles for the whole life of society and of the world.

But here again there were elements of uncertainty in the witness. The basic concept of Stockholm remained unclear. It had been decided to exclude all doctrinal issues from the deliberations. Now in order to justify that decision arguments were used which seemed to imply a denial of the need for any common starting point or any common conviction concerning the nature of Christian unity. Thus the Executive Committee stated in 1922 that 'doctrine divides, but service unites'.[24] But is it not precisely the characteristic of Christian universalism that its centre is the one whom Christians confess to be the agent of unity, so that the affirmation (which is of course doctrinal) that he is the divine Saviour and the response to his call in service are both indispensable elements of Christian universalism? There were a number of prominent Stockholm delegates who considered it the greatest merit of the conference that it had discovered a unity which was not based on any specific common affirmation of faith, but on a common life, and thus made Stockholm appear as a victory for the type of ecumenism which was so broad that it had neither a clear centre nor recognizable frontiers.

It must be added that some Stockholm leaders confused

[24] Letter to Gardiner from the Executive Committee in August 1922.

the picture by organizing immediately after the Stockholm Conference a movement called the 'Universal Religious Peace Conference' which stated that it did not want to mix the religions, but did in fact move toward syncretism by publishing a book of devotions taken from the scriptures of all religions.

It is probable that the aggressive Encyclical *'Mortalium Animos'* of 1928, in which the Vatican described the ecumenical movement as a body of complete relativists who considered that 'all religions are more or less good and praiseworthy', was at least partly based on impressions from such sources. That was of course a caricature and showed that the Vatican had not really studied the conference documents. Those documents make it clear that Söderblom and the vast majority of the delegates took their stand on a Christocentric foundation. The Message of the Conference had made this clear when it said: 'The nearer we draw to the Crucified, the nearer we come to one another. . . . In the Crucified and Risen Lord alone lies the world's hope.' Stockholm gave in fact a clearer Christian witness than its unsatisfactory underlying theory seemed to imply.

In the twelve years between the Life and Work Conferences of Stockholm and of Oxford a great change took place in the theological climate. The emergence of a new biblical theology, the influence of Karl Barth, the challenge of totalitarianism and the new emphasis on the Church as an inherent part of the Christian message, made it inevitable that the 1937 conference should think of unity in new terms.

Once again a layman became the central figure in the ecumenical movement. For it was Dr J. H. Oldham who in the thirties laid the foundations, not only of the Oxford Conference of 1937, but also of the World Council of Churches. His great passion was to make the Christian faith relevant to the modern world. He spent a great deal of his time and energy on discovering what laymen in different spheres of life were thinking. One wonders whether at that time anyone else had such a comprehensive knowledge of what was going on in the minds of scientists and sociologists, philosophers and authors. But as he reflected on the answer to be given to their questions, he came more and more to the conclusion laid down in these words: 'Either the Christian affirmation holds good, that God has disclosed his nature, his Will, his purpose in Christ, so that those who respond to the revelation are united in a new, divinely-created and divinely-sustained order of life, *or* man is left to his own vague, uncertain and conflicting intuitions and surmises of the divine.'[25] And he saw that between this Christocentric universality and the new political universal ideologies there was an irreconcilable opposition. It was due to this insight, shared by many others, that the Oxford Conference gave a good witness over against the idolatries of the time and helped mightily to lay the spiritual foundations for the future of the ecumenical movement.

Thus 'Life and Work' and 'Faith and Order' had by 1937 both moved toward a deeper and wider conception of Christian universalism. It was more generally understood that the ecumenical movement would have to be definitely Christocentric, that it would have to be a movement of re-discovery and renewal of the Church, but not of the Church as an aim in itself, rather of the Church as the chosen instrument for the world-embracing saving work of Christ.

Thus it was natural for these movements to decide together the formation of the World Council of Churches. In 1938 at Utrecht the constitution for the new World Council was drawn up and it was decided to take the basis which had so far been that of Faith and Order alone, as the basis for the World Council itself. William Temple explained that decision as follows: 'It (the Basis) is an affirma-

[25] *The Student World*, 1935, p. 376.

tion of the Incarnation and the Atonement. The Council desires to be a fellowship of those churches which accept these truths.'[26]

Was this Christian universalism only theory? That was the great question to be answered when the Second World War broke out. The Oxford message had said: 'If war breaks out, then pre-eminently the Church must be the Church, still united as the Body of Christ, though the nations wherein it is planted fight each other.' To a very real extent this promise was fulfilled and the war years, instead of destroying or weakening the ecumenical movement, became the time when the reality of the Christian fellowship transcending all divisions became more clear than ever before. It was a fellowship which found its nurture in the common confession of loyalty to the one Lord over against the lords of the new and idolatrous ideologies.

At the time of the official inauguration of the World Council of Churches this Christocentric view of the Council's character was reaffirmed. The first Assembly in 1948 described 'our given unity' in the words: 'God has given to his people in Jesus Christ a unity which is his creation and not our achievement.'[27] And when the Council sought to define its own character in 1950 (Toronto) it added: 'The Basis of the World Council is the acknowledgment of the central fact that "other foundation can no man lay than that is laid, even Jesus Christ". It is the expression of the conviction that the Lord of the Church is God-among-us who continues to gather his children and to build his Church himself.'[28]

In the further development of the Council it has become increasingly clear that this concentration on the central affirmation of the faith was the only right orientation for

[26] Explanatory Memorandum of 1938.
[27] Official Report. First Assembly of the WCC, p. 51.
[28] Workbook for the New Delhi Assembly, p. 65.

the ecumenical movement. That is why the Evanston Assembly had as its theme 'Jesus Christ—the Hope of the World', and the New Delhi Assembly the theme 'Jesus Christ, the Light of the World'. And that is why the Lund Conference on Faith and Order found that the central subject for ecumenical discussion had to be: 'Christ and the Church.'

But even this was not yet the complete witness that the churches were called to make. As long as there were two councils, one concerned with the co-operation and unity of the churches, another with missions, the double misunderstanding was possible that unity could mean a unity sought for the sake of the Church alone and that missions were a specialized activity outside the normal life of the Church. The ecumenical movement had to show that the 'one' and 'the many' belonged together. And this could only be done as the World Council of Churches and the International Missionary Council (which had already entered into close association with each other) became fully integrated. It was therefore providential that in recent years in both bodies there had developed a strong conviction that they belonged together. Unity was to be understood as unity for the sake of the universal mission of the Church. Universality was to be understood as the *raison d'être* of unity. And both found their centre in the one divine Lord. So at New Delhi in 1961 the World Council of Churches and the International Missionary Council became one body.

At the New Delhi Assembly two other events took place which have a bearing on the World Council's conception of universalism. The first was that the Basis of the Council was expanded. In the new formula the confession of the Lord Jesus Christ as God and Saviour is clarified by the words 'according to the Scriptures'. It is in the Jesus Christ who came into history and to whom the Scriptures bear witness that the churches find their common foundation.

It was also stated that the churches seek to fulfil their common calling to the glory of the one God, Father, Son and Holy Spirit. The Council is Christocentric, but precisely because it is Christocentric it must be Trinitarian.

The other event was the adoption of a statement which defines what the unity is which the churches in the Council seek and which makes clear that that unity is not some vague, intangible unity, but a concrete, visible unity manifested in each place.

Thus by the time of the New Delhi Assembly the Council had been led step by step to work out the full implications of a specifically Christian universalism: the rootage in the common confession of the one Saviour, the concern for the unity and obedience of his people, the calling to bring the word of salvation and the ministry of reconciliation to all men everywhere.

The answer to syncretism is not introversion, a turning away from the world of religions and cultures fearing that they might contaminate the purity of the Christian message. The answer to syncretism is to enter into that world with the Gospel of the one Saviour who has come for all men everywhere and to do this with the faith that that Gospel, if faithfully obeyed, will itself maintain its purity.

What then are the implications of such an answer to syncretism?

(a) *Implications for the nature of a true universalism*

The Christian Church must make it unmistakably clear that it believes in a universalism which has its one and only centre in the work of Jesus Christ. At this point there must be no compromise of any kind. We cannot participate in the search for a common denominator of all the religions, because the one foundation has been laid and the edifice of humanity comes tumbling down when that foundation is undermined. But that does not mean that the universalism of the Christian Church is a universalism concerned only with the Christian part of humanity. Too often the churches have given that wrong impression. Too often they have defended Christian interests alone. But the Church does not exist for the sake of the Church. It exists for the sake of humanity. Karl Barth[29] has put this truth in a provocative form. He says that we must dare to affirm that while the world would be lost without Jesus Christ, the world would not be lost without the Church. For who would prevent him from going his own direct way to men? But the Church would be lost without humanity. For if the Church should try to be the Church without caring for humanity, it would depart from Jesus Christ who is the Saviour of all men.

It is a strange fact that the Church and the theologians have left it to the humanistic philosophers, to the free-masons, to theosophists or Bahaists to raise the issue of the unity of mankind. Many widely used treatises of Christian ethics deal fully with the problems of the Christian attitude to the family or to the state but, if they deal at all with humanity, it is in order to warn against a romantic humani-tarianism. Not so the New Testament. In it the perspective of humanity is always present. The whole New Testament proclamation is characterized by an 'exuberant joy in the universality of Christ'.[30] This finds expression in the very frequent use of the words 'all' and (meaning basically the same) 'many'. Christ has died for all, for the reconciliation of the world. The Lord identifies himself with all his suffer-ing brethren (Matt. 25). The good news is to be carried to all men. On the last day all the nations will be gathered before his glorious throne.

The more seriously the Christian Church takes its centre, the more universal it becomes. The point has been stated clearly by a great servant of humanity, Dag Hammar-

---

[29] *Church Dogmatics* IV, 3.2, ET, 1962, p. 826.
[30] B. Reicke in *TWNT* V, p. 895 (*pas, hapas*).

skjöld, when Secretary General of the United Nations. Speaking to the Evanston Assembly of the World Council of Churches he quoted the following words from the Report on the Main Theme of the Assembly : 'The Cross is that place at the centre of the world's history . . . where all men and all nations without exception stand revealed as enemies of God . . . and yet where all men stand revealed as beloved of God, precious in God's sight.' Mr Hammarskjöld continued : 'So understood, the Cross, although it is the unique fact on which the Christian churches base their hope, should not separate those of the Christian faith from others, but should instead be that element in their lives which enables them to stretch out their hands to peoples of other creeds in the feeling of universal brotherhood which we hope one day to see reflected in a world of nations truly united.'[31]

The alternative between a Christianity so totally preoccupied by the original central revelation that it forgets the concerns and needs of humanity and a Christianity so obsessed with the interests of humanity that it becomes uprooted, is a false alternative. In the Bible we are forced by the dynamism inherent in the centre to go out to the circumference, but our contact with the circumference throws us back on the centre. It is therefore misleading to say, as Floyd H. Ross says, that the great issue of the hour is not Christian ecumenism, but human ecumenism.[32] For ecumenism is not really Christian if it is not concerned with humanity and a human ecumenism which is not rooted in the fact of Christ is not a true ecumenism, but a vague humanitarianism without a centre and without a foundation.

[31] *Ecumenical Review*, July 1956, p. 402.
[32] In *The Theology of the Christian Mission*, edited by G. H. Anderson, 1961, p. 214.

(b) *Implications for our attitude to the religions*

The attitude of the Christian Church to the religions can therefore only be the attitude of the witness who points to the one Lord Jesus Christ as Lord of all men. Where the Church ceases to give this witness, it ceases to have a *raison d'être*, for it came into being to proclaim this good news and not to add one more form of spiritual experience to the many which existed already.

The Christian Church cannot therefore participate in the search for a synthesis or confluence of the existing religions. Such a combination would not be an enrichment for humanity, for it could only be achieved by treating the religions as human ideologies of which man himself is the centre. And it would mean that the Christian Church had given up its identity and integrity.

The Church does not apologize for the fact that it wants all men to know Jesus Christ and to follow him. Its very calling is to proclaim the Gospel to the ends of the earth. It cannot make any restrictions in this respect. Whether people have a high, a low or a primitive religion, whether they have sublime ideals or a defective morality makes no fundamental difference in this respect. All must hear the Gospel: Greeks with their rich philosophical tradition; yes and even the Jews with whom the Christians have so much in common and to whom they owe so much.

It is difficult to understand that so many philosophers of religion and historians interpret this missionary attitude of the Church in terms of a complex of superiority. No one can deny that Western Christianity has very often given the impression that it looked down on other religions and considered itself as the proud possessor of the truth. And it is therefore understandable that those who know little of the foundations of Christianity consider Christians as arrogant and narrow-minded. But one would expect that serious students of religion and history would discover that the claim which the Church makes for its Lord has its origin, not in any religious or cultural egocentricity, but in the message of the New Testament itself. For the whole New Testament speaks of the Saviour whom we have not chosen, but who has chosen us. It is possible to reject him, but it is not seriously possible to think of him as one of the many prophets or founders of religion. A Christianity which should think of itself as one of many diverse contributions to the religious life of mankind is a Christianity that has lost its foundation in the New Testament.

Does that mean that the Christian Church must always take the attitude of monologue and that there is no place for any form of dialogue between Christians and non-Christians? Our answer would have to be affirmative, if dialogue left no room for witness. But that is not the case. Martin Buber, who has given us what is probably the most profound analysis of the nature of dialogue, has made it very clear that the presupposition of genuine dialogue is not that the partners agree beforehand to relativize their own convictions, but that they accept each other as persons.[33] In order to enter into a deep relationship with a person the essential requirement is not that he agrees with me, that I agree with him or that we both are willing to negotiate a compromise, but rather that I turn to him with the willingness to listen to him, to understand him, to seek mutual enrichment. I do not impose my personality on him but put myself at his disposal with all that I am. As a Christian I cannot do this without reporting to him what I have come to know about Jesus Christ. I shall make clear that I consider my faith not as an achievement, but as a gift of grace, a gift which excludes all pride, but which obliges me to speak gratefully of this Lord to all who will hear it. I shall be glad also to listen to my partner and may

[33] *Schriften über das dialogische Prinzip*, Heidelberg, 1954, p. 279.

learn much from his account of his spiritual journey. The dialogue will be all the richer, if both of us give ourselves as we are. For the Christian that giving must include witness. It is possible for convinced Christians to enter into true dialogue with convinced Hindus or Muslims or Jews, yes and even syncretists, without giving up their basic conviction. It should be done in the attitude which Hocking has so well defined as 'reverence for reverence'.[34] The fact that Christians believe that they know the source of divine truth does not mean that they have nothing to learn from men of other faiths. Those of us who have had the privilege of participating in such conversations have often found ourselves humbled and challenged by the evidence we have seen of true devotion, of unflinching loyalty to the truth as they see it among adherents of other religions. And on both sides it has often been found more worth while to have conversations with men of definite convictions rather than with men of uncertain and vague opinions.

But does it not remain true that the acceptance of the uniqueness of the Christian Gospel leads to intolerance? That depends on the meaning we attach to that word. If it is intolerance to believe that there is only one Saviour who has come for all men, then Christians must accept the accusation of intolerance. But if it means that the Christian Church does not recognize the right of the various religions to enjoy the same freedom which the Church asks for itself, then the answer must be quite different. It is of course true that during long periods of history (and unfortunately still to-day in some countries) many churches have claimed freedom for themselves without being willing to grant it to others. To-day the situation has changed. Many churches have learned their hard lessons and have come to understand that the use of other than purely spiritual means in the encounter of religions is unworthy of the Gospel. The

[34] *The Coming World Civilisation*, p. 154.

third Assembly of the World Council of Churches in 1961 has put this in clear language: 'Christians see religious liberty as a consequence of God's creative work, of his redemption of man in Christ and his calling of men into his service. God's redemptive dealing with men is not coercive. Accordingly human attempts by legal enactment or by pressure of social custom to coerce or to eliminate faith are violations of the fundamental ways of God with men. The freedom which God has given in Christ implies a free response to God's love, and the responsibility to serve fellow-men at the point of deepest need. Holding a distinctive Christian basis for religious liberty, we regard this right as fundamental for men everywhere.'[35] This means of course that the basic right of each religion to carry on missionary activity is recognized, and that the answer of the Christian churches to such activity on the part of the religions must not be the recourse to any form of legal, political or social pressure, but only the spiritual answer of their witness. The coming great encounter of the religions must be a purely spiritual encounter.

(c) *Implications for collaboration in common tasks*

The structure of modern national and international society is such that many problems of a cultural, social, political and international character can only be solved through large-scale collaboration of all existing organizations, including the churches. So the churches are constantly confronted with the question whether they are ready to co-operate with other bodies, and this raises especially the issue of interreligious co-operation. Such co-operation is possible and desirable on two conditions.

The first is that it be made clear that it is undertaken to achieve specific common purposes and not to render common witness to common religious convictions. There is

[35] *The New Delhi Report*, pp. 159-60.

everything to be said for having bodies representing different faiths take a common stand on great public issues and work together in the fields of social work or international relations. Far more could be done in this field than is yet being done. But there is nothing to be said for giving the mistaken impression that such collaboration implies that the differences between these bodies are in fact of secondary importance. Interreligious co-operation does not necessarily imply the acceptance of syncretism. It will lead to the creation of a syncretistic atmosphere, if the partners concerned by their statements or by their silence create the misunderstanding that the practical tasks on which they agree are the really important matters and that the differences between the various religions have only to do with 'the details of orthodoxy'. But it is also possible to engage together on common tasks with a clear understanding that the co-operating bodies differ in their basic convictions and that their working together does not in any way mean that they relativize their deepest faith.

In most cases this will mean that interreligious co-operation should be concerned with clearly defined and limited tasks. The problem becomes more difficult if the common task to be undertaken has to do with long-range issues of a cultural character including the realm of education and of national and international ethos or ideology. For it is impossible to work out policies in these fields without opting for a certain conception of man, and the question: 'What think ye of man?' is finally based on the question: 'What think ye of God?' It can easily happen that Christians who enter into co-operation with men of other faiths in such areas find that, in spite of their intention to remain completely loyal to their convictions, they are caught in what is in fact an attempt to proclaim a faith above all faiths which embraces and at the same time smothers all historical religions.

But here again it is not impossible to avoid the syncretistic temptation. An important example is the 'Universal Declaration of Human Rights' adopted by the General Assembly of the United Nations in 1948. That declaration was worked out by a commission of which the membership was formed by men of very different religious background. It bears the marks of being a composite document and uses at certain points ambiguous language. A document written from the point of view of one single religion would of course have greater unity and precision. But it has the great advantage of saying no more than what men of so many different faiths can say together without betraying their real convictions and without pretending that they are ultimately agreed in their basic standpoints concerning the destiny of man. Thus it is not a syncretistic document, but a modest attempt to state what the majoriy of nations can say together about human rights. In this way it is a useful contribution to the creation of an international ethos and deserves, in spite of its obvious weaknesses, to be taken more seriously than it has yet been taken.

The second condition is that such co-operation must not draw an artificial line of demarcation between those who call themselves religious and those who do not. The distinction is artificial because there does not exist a common definition of religion. The temptation is therefore to include all those who call themselves religious and to exclude those who do not. But this leads to a most arbitrary grouping. Christians or Christian churches have no good reason to associate themselves with every group which calls itself religious over against those who do not. There is no point in creating a front in which the churches would find themselves allied with representatives of religion from the most sublime to the most superstitious and idolatrous against idealists, agnostics and humanists who prefer not to call themselves religious. There are forms of modern secularism which in the light of biblical norms mean spiritual advance rather than retrogression. A common front of all religions against the non-religious could only make our present confusion worse. It would on the one hand confirm the wrong impression that what we stand for is a religion within and behind the existing religions. It would on the other hand widen the gulf between the churches and the secular world. If we co-operate with men of other religions it must not be to defend all that is said and done in the name of religion, but rather to defend together with all who are willing to participate the interests of man against his old enemies: hunger, disease, oppression, injustice.

As the dialogue of the religions, the critical importance of which Dr Hendrik Kraemer has described in his *World Cultures and World Religions*, gets under way, the churches will be called upon more and more frequently to co-operate with men of other faiths and of no faith in matters of public life. We will have to accept that new duty. We must become imaginative in discovering how in the pluriform national societies, and in the even more pluriform international society, we may be able to take common action with others in relation to such burning issues as racial justice, family life, rapid social change and the creation of international order. But we will have to make it perfectly plain that our willingness to co-operate does not in any way imply a willingness to compromise on the basic issues of the faith.

(d) *Implications for the communication of the Gospel*

Communication always implies the use of concepts, thought-forms and terminology which are comprehensible to those with whom one wants to communicate. There is therefore no effective Christian witness which is not in a certain sense a translation into categories which differ from the categories used in the original kerygma. All missionary witness implies accommodation or transformation.

It has been suggested that we must therefore admit that all theologies are inevitably syncretistic. Thus Professor Russell Chandran says that every Christian theology contains some syncretism and that the West should acknowledge that its theology is also syncretistic, in so far as it arose always and everywhere in a specific framework.[36] It seems to me that in this and similar statements the word syncretism is not used in the right way. A theology is not syncretistic if and when it uses the thought-forms of the environment in which it operates. A theology becomes syncretistic if and when in using such thought-forms it introduces into its structure ideas which change the meaning of biblical truth in its substance.

This distinction is essential. It is one thing to accommodate the Gospel to a specific culture or to translate it in a specific terminology and to do this with real loyalty to the original message. It is another thing to mix the biblical revelation with categories of thought which transform that revelation into something else than it is. And we must not use the same word for these two processes. We can agree with Professor Chandran that every theology contains the danger of syncretism. We must also agree that Western theology has very often, in seeking to accommodate the Christian message to the Western cultural environment, distorted its substance and thus become syncretistic. But that does not mean that we must resign ourselves to the fact that syncretism is inevitable.

The thesis of this book is that syncretism is not inevitable. This has been proved by St Paul and St John. They had to translate the original Gospel into the categories of thought and the terminology of a new environment. They have done so without becoming syncretistic, without changing the

[36] In *Evangelisches Missions-Magazin* 1961, No. 3, p. 98.

nature of the basic witness. They have done so with an astonishing freedom and courage and taken very great risks. But they have remained faithful.

We must try to regain something of the same freedom and courage. We must believe that it is not only possible but absolutely necessary to interpret the Gospel in terms which will bring it closer to the cultures in which up till now it has been generally proclaimed in a Western and therefore foreign form. It is clear that this cannot be done overnight. It is also clear that real risks are involved. But our desire to arrive at a truly adequate communication of the Gospel must be stronger than our fear of syncretism. Where there is a deep loyalty to the revelation, that revelation itself will overcome the hindrances and keep us from falling into the temptation of cheap and false forms of adaptation. The time has come when the 'multi-coloured' wisdom of God must express itself in new Asian and African expressions of Christian thought and life.

(e) *Implications for the life of the Church*

Finally we must once more emphasize that all our affirmations about Christocentric universalism will be meaningless and our rejection of syncretism will be of little avail if we do not practise that universalism in the life of the Church. So far we have practised it very little. Our lack of unity and the slowness of our progress toward unity are precisely due to the fact that we express our faith in the *'Una Sancta'*, but act as if the Church were our holy denominational Church. And our situation is all the more serious since we have now made it so clear to the world and to ourselves that it is in the nature of the Church to be one and universal.

Kraemer's analysis of the coming dialogue of the world religions ends with this sentence: 'The Christian Church . . . should first and foremost set her own house in order, because the greatest service she can render to the world, the Western and the Eastern world, is by being resolutely the Church of Jesus Christ.'[37] Newbigin's discussion of the faith for this one world of ours concludes that 'nothing is more central to the missionary task of the Church to-day than this—that there should be a recovery of the visible unity of Christians, that men of every race and culture may be able to recognize in the Church the authentic lineaments of the household of God, the home in which every man is invited to be reborn as a child of the one Father and a brother of the Son of Man'.[38] We have been led to the same conclusion.

The ecumenical movement is the expression of a new understanding of the Church as the people of God, Christ-centred and therefore universal. We have also the beginnings of a relationship between the churches which expresses this insight. But the main task of transforming our churches into that Church Universal which they are meant to be lies still before us.

That we really believe that there is a unity in Christ such as nowhere else can only be truly demonstrated by acts of unity, by overcoming our divisions. That we really believe that Christ is the Saviour of all can only become a convincing faith, if the Church breaks out of its too introverted life, shows clearly its concern for the spiritual and physical needs of all men and manifests that it is not a national, an ideological, a racial or a continental church, but the Church Universal which is at home in every nation and yet does not belong to any nation.

The only effective answer to syncretism is the demonstration in word and deed that the quest of humanity for oneness finds its fulfilment in the mystery of the Son of God who came to give his life for all men.

[37] *World Cultures and World Religions*, 1960.
[38] *A Faith for this one World?*, pp. 125f.

INDEX OF NAMES

Abraham, 15
Adam, 97f.
Adhyar, 43
Adonis, 13, 21, 51, 69
Aedesius, 16
Africa, 45, 47
Ahurah Mazda, 38
Akbar, 36, 87
Albright, W. F., 66
Alexander of Abouno-
    teichos, 17
Alexander the Great,
    14f.
Alexander Severus, 15
Allah, 37
Althaus, P., 98
Altheim, F., 19
America, 26, 29
Ammonius Saccas, 42
Amsterdam, 111
Anderson, G. H., 115
Antioch, 51, 65
Antipas, 61
Antony, Mark, 52
Aphrodite, 53
Apollo, 27, 51
Apollonius of Tyana,
    15, 52
Apuleius, 15, 17, 53
Artemis, 51f., 56f.
Asklepios, 60f.
Assyria, 12f.
Astarte 13, 51, 55
Athens, 57
Attis, 15, 21, 69, 81
Augustine, 14, 20, 77
Augustus, 52f., 60
Aurelian, 19, 87

Baal, 51
Babbitt, I., 23
Babylonia, 12ff., 50
Bach, J. S., 83
Baha' U'llah, Bahai, 35,
    43, 88, 114
Balaam, 61
Barth, K., 40, 94f., 103,
    114
Baruch, 81
Behm, J., 73
Berdyaev, N., 91, 93
Berlin, 62
Bertoli, D., 36
Bidez, J., 18
Binyon, L., 36
Blauw, J., 99
Blavatsky, Mme H. P.,
    42
Boissier, G., 16, 22
Bornkamm, G., 69
Bousset, W., 65, 78
Brahma, 38
Brazil, 47
Brent, C. H., 105f.
Britain, 15
Brunner, E., 40
Buber, M., 117
Buchman, F., 48
Buddhism, 21, 35, 38,
    44f., 85, 88
Bultmann, R., 12, 72, 77

Cadbury, H. J., 53
Camargo, C. P. de, 47
Cao Dai, 44
Carlyle, T., 26

Ceres, 17f.
Chaitanya, 37
Chandran, R., 123
Chartres, 33
Chicago, 35, 37f., 43
China, 20
Claudius, 50
Colossae, 58ff., 94
Confucius, 44f.
Corinth, 51, 53
Cullmann, O., 73, 98
Cumont, F., 14ff., 19f.,
    54
Cybele, 15f., 69

Daniel, 69
Daniélou, J., 66
Davey, N., 73
Demeter, 17, 69
Demetrius, 56f.
Descartes, R., 44
Diana, 18, 25
Dibelius, M., 58ff., 94
Diocletian, 20
Dionysos Sabazios, 15,
    60
Dionysus, 17, 19, 27,
    52, 69
Dodd, C. H., 65, 74
Döllinger, J. J. I., 51
Dostoievski, F., 83

Edinburgh, 103ff., 107
Egypt, 14f., 18, 50, 54
Eisenhower, D. D., 49
Eleusis, 18, 32, 69, 81

Emerson, R. W., 26
Emesa, 19
Ephesus, 51ff., 56f., 82
Eusebius, 53
Evanston, 112, 115
Ezekiel, 13

Farquhar, J. N., 37f.
Faust, 14, 24ff.
France, 26, 47

Gama, Vasco da, 29
Gandhi, 39
Gardiner, R., 106, 108
Gaugler, E., 72
Germany, 15, 26, 40
Gibbon, E., 49
Goethe, J. W., 24ff., 28, 46
Grant, R. M., 21, 71, 81
El Greco, 83
Greece, 27, 50ff.
Grundmann, W., 55
Guadelupe, 33
Gunkel, H., 77f.

Hammarskjöld, D., 114f.
Harnack, A. von, 12, 76, 78ff.
Hecate, 16ff., 52
Helena, 25, 55, 81
Heracles, 27
Herberg, W., 49
Hierocles, 53
Hocking, W. E., 33ff., 87f., 118
Hölderlin, F., 26ff.
Holmes, J. H., 95
Hooke, S. H., 13
Hoskyns, E. C., 73
Houghton, W. R., 38
Huber, M., 87
Hugo, Victor, 44

Hutten, K., 46
Huxley, A., 89f.

Inayat Khan, 44
India, 36ff.
Iran, *see* Persia
Irenaeus, 51, 71, 74, 81
Isaiah, 66
Isis, 17, 30, 51, 69

Japan, 44f.
Jeanne d'Arc, 44
Jeremiah, 13
Jeremias, J., 100
Jerome, 52
Jerusalem, 12f., 50
Jesus Christ, *passim*
John Evangelist, St, 53, 66, 71f., 75, 78, 123
John of the Cross, St, 33
Joubert, J., 23
Julian the Apostate, 15, 18, 77, 87
Jung, C. G., 31f., 91
Justin the Gnostic, 81
Justin Martyr, 51, 55

Kardec, A., 47
Keshab, Chandra Sen, 37
Kittel, G., 63
Kraemer, H., 11, 122, 124f.
Krishna, 44

Laeuchli, S., 81f.
Lake, K., 53
Lao Tse, 32, 44
Latte, K., 16f.
Lawrence, D. H., 30, 91
Leadbeater, C. W., 45f.
Leisegang, H., 81
Lietzmann, H., 14, 16, 19, 21, 50, 73f., 80f.

Los Angeles, 48
Lucian, 51
Lucius, 17, 53
Luhan, Mabel D., 30
Lystra, 57

Maiumas, 51
Manasseh, 12
Manetho, 18
Mani, Manicheism, 20f., 77
Manson, T. W., 13
Marx, K., 95
Melkart, 53
Michel, 66
Mithra, Mithraism, 15, 17, 19f., 63
Mohammed, 33, 44
Moses, 12, 33, 47
Mother Goddess, 18, 51ff.
Mott, J. R., 39, 103, 105
Mozart, 83

Naassenes, 21, 70f., 81
Nebuchadnezzar, 69
Needham, J., 84ff.
Nehru, J., 38f.
New Delhi, 111ff., 119
Newbigin, J. L., 34f., 125
Nock, A. D., 14ff., 18, 76f.
Northrop, F. S. C., 33, 35

Oepke, A., 11, 63, 98, 102
Oldham, J. H., 109f.
Oomoto, 44f.
Orion, 45f.
Orpheus, 15
Osiris, 21
Oxford, 108, 111

Panikkar, K. M., 29, 86
Paul, St, *passim*
Percy, E., 58
Pergamon, 6of.
Persia, 15, 44, 50, 54
Phillips, D. B., 32
Philostratos, 52
Plato, 81
Pliny, 76
Plutarch, 50, 63
Porphyry, 77
Praetextatus, 16
Preiss, T., 103
Preuschen, E., 53
Prümm, K., 14
Ptolemaeus, 71
Ptolemy I, 18, 87
Purucker, G. de, 43
Pythagoras, 81

Quispel, G., 55
Qumran, 65ff., 69, 71

Radhakrishnan, S., 39f., 87
Ramakrishna Paraham-sa, 36f., 39, 41
Ramsay, W. M., 57
Rembrandt, 83
Reicke, B., 114
Renan, E., 51
Rolland, R., 37ff., 42
Rome, 15f., 51, 53f., 60

Ross, F. L., 115
Rousseau, J.-J., 23f., 28

Sabazios, *see* Dionysos
Samaria, 54ff.
Sarapis, 18
Schäferdiek, 61
Schleiermacher, F. E. D., 94
Schmidt, K. L., 72
Schmitz, O., 61
Schultze, S., 106
Sell, K., 25
Shakespeare, 83
Shamas, 13
Shiva, 37
Simon Magus, 51, 54ff., 81
Söderblom, N., 107, 109
Soest, 106
Stael, Mme de, 23, 26
Stählin, G., 64
Stählin, W., 46
Steiner, R., 46
Stockholm, 107ff.
Sundkler, B., 45
Symmachus, 23, 35
Syria, 15, 54

Tambaram, 104
Tammuz, 13
Temple, W., 111
Teno-san, 45

Thomsen, H., 45
Timotheus, 18
Tonneau, R., 51f.
Toronto, 111
Townshend, G., 43
Toynbee, A., 34f.
Trajan, 76
Turchi, N., 18

Umbanda, 47
Utrecht, 110

Vestdijk, S., 31f.
Vietnam, 44
Vincent, L.-H., 55
Vivekenanda, S., 37ff., 41
Voltaire, 23

Weil, S., 93
Wendland, P., 14, 17, 63
Whitman, W., 29
Williams, D. R., 95
Wilmette, 33

Yahweh, 12, 33, 38, 60

Zarathustra, 46
Zeus, 19, 60, 81
Zoroaster, 21, 38